HOME ON THE FARM

ESSAYS ON A MICHIGAN CHILDHOOD

BY JERRY R. DAVIS

*To a fellow Traveler,
Erik,*

Jerry R. Davis

ISBN: 1-4107-7939-4 (e-book)
ISBN: 1-4107-7938-6 (Paperback)
ISBN: 1-4107-7937-8 (Dust Jacket)

Library of Congress Control Number: 2003095705

This book is printed on acid free paper.

Printed in the United States of America
Bloomington, IN

1st Books - rev. 09/16/03

Dedication

I would like to dedicate this book to my mother,

Ernestine V. Davis (Williamson)

Though she wrote all her life, she never completed her book.

ACKNOWLEDGMENTS

I wish to thank all the people who made this book possible. Ron Baldwin and Mary Milford spent many hours proofreading the manuscript. Laurel Davis, Joanne Inman, Dan Davis, Gene Seney, Vickie Kilbourne, Bonnie Seney, Carrie Smart and Geraldine Liebknecht provided factual information when my own memory failed me. Jay Dirago and Chuck Qualley made many useful suggestions for additions to the manuscript. Curt Caylor, Steve Lucero and Jerry Ginsburg assisted by helping me overcome my technical inadequacy with the computer for which I am most grateful.

PROLOGUE

Home on the Farm is my first attempt to write a book. All my previous writing took the form of short papers or articles. When I was earning my Master's degree in history at Central Michigan University, I wrote a number of research papers on various historical subjects, but none of them compared in length to this manuscript. Here is the evolution of my book.

During my three decade career in education, I taught American history in various junior high schools in central Michigan. Each year as we covered the settlers' movement into the Midwest and beyond, I would describe episodes about my childhood on the farm to my history classes. I remember how fascinated the students seemed with them. If blasé eighth graders found them interesting, then it seemed possible that those stories could have wider appeal than I had previously imagined. Perhaps they could be written as individual self-contained vignettes and put together to form a book about growing up in rural Michigan.

Next it behooved me to actually begin putting something down on paper—or in this electronic age—on the computer. I started by making a list of twenty or so proposed chapter topics. That was an interesting and nostalgic stroll into my past, and I enjoyed taking it. I found that when I began to really think *in depth* about my childhood, memories slowly began to emerge. As I continued, they came to me faster and faster, until finally I was literally awash in mental images of my life as a child! New subjects for additional chapters occur to me almost daily, and that original list of twenty topics now has grown to over thirty-five. Perhaps I'll write about all of them, but more than likely some will be ignored. After all, I should save some material for a sequel!

When my list of proposed topics was assembled, I looked it over very carefully in order to determine which one I wanted to elaborate on first. I selected the topic of the traveling salesman and the new kitchen range and began to write. Soon I became so engrossed in the effort that I forgot my surroundings completely, and didn't finish it until well after midnight. I actually had made a start! The first six pages of my book were written! In the interim, those six pages have been altered, rewritten, edited and proofread until they hardly resemble the original, but they remain my first six pages nonetheless. Some of the later chapters were easier to write than the first and some were harder, but writing each of them has given me much pleasure.

The chapters are divided into seven groupings, beginning with *Roots,* which includes chapters on both my paternal and maternal grandparents, and continuing through *Parents, Siblings, Others, Schooling, Surroundings, and Animals.* One grouping contains only one chapter, but three of them have six chapters each.

This is not a chronological story of my childhood. The reader will find that in telling my story through certain topics, it was occasionally necessary to go forward or backward in time. The narrative is filled with flashbacks and flashforwards—hopefully, they do not confuse the reader. My intent was that they would do just the opposite—that is, to make the subject clear and easy to understand. Here is a bare bones chronology of my youth: I was born in 1932 on our farm near Tuscola, Michigan. When I was nine years old and in the fifth grade, we moved to the farm near Vassar. I lived there until I was graduated from high school in 1949 and entered Michigan State University as a freshman.

I have tried to make each essay/chapter a complete story unto itself. They could be read and understood individually without reading the others. However, in order to learn the total story, it is necessary for the reader to peruse all of them. If your goal is something other than that, then read as few or as many of the vignettes as you wish. I'll be pleased and gratified if you read and enjoy only one of them.

Jerry R. Davis, July 2001

Albuquerque, New Mexico

CHAPTER TITLES

MICHIGAN

TUSCOLA COUNTY

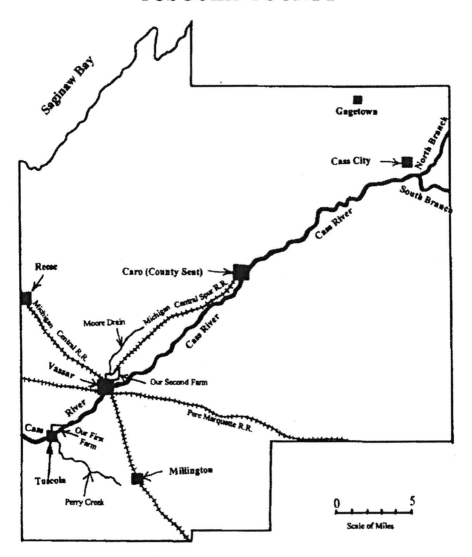

Saginaw Bay

Gagetown

Cass City → North Branch

South Branch

Reese

Caro (County Seat)

Cass River

Michigan Central Spur R.R.

Moore Drain

Michigan Central R.R.

Cass River

Vassar

Our Second Farm

River

Pere Marquette R.R.

Cass

Our First Farm

Tuscola

Millington

Perry Creek

0   5

Scale of Miles

CHAPTER 1

AN UNLIKELY COUPLE

AN UNLIKELY COUPLE

She was a beautiful teenager. Her family, composed of parents, one brother and two sisters, lived on an isolated eighty-acre farm. Recently, after attending a nearby one-room school, she was graduated from the eighth grade. He was a balding man in his mid-thirties and the father of a school-age son and an infant daughter. The baby's birth had come at a high price. That price was the young mother's life. What could the widower and the girl possibly have in common, other than being nodding acquaintances when meeting in their daily rounds of activities? They were a most unlikely couple.

The widower was my dad's father, William Davis. He was born during the Civil War on November 21, 1864, just six days after General Sherman began his famous "march to the sea" from Atlanta to Savannah. It is likely that Grandpa's family and neighbors at that time were unaware of the Georgia campaign which did so much to determine the war's outcome. William was the fifth child of James Hervey and Frances Maria (Weldon) Davis who owned a farm on the north bank of the Cass River. It was a couple of miles west of the Village of Tuscola in the southwestern corner of Tuscola County.

The Davis family had one small claim to fame. They were the direct descendants of Ebenezer and Phebe Davis who were known as the first permanent white settlers of Tuscola County. The reason that "permanent" is underscored is that there was one settler who arrived nearly six months earlier than the Davises did, but he stayed only a short time and then moved on. In contrast, once the Davises moved to the county, they lived there the rest of their lives. Those first settlers were my grandfather's grandparents, thus they were my great great grandparents.

On Grandpa Davis's twenty-fourth birthday in 1888 he married a nineteen year old neighbor girl, Amelia Hustler, who was known as "Millie". Together they bought a small farm a few miles away from the Davis homestead and settled down to raise a family. The next year a son, Earl, was born and they were well on their way. I have a picture of the three of them taken shortly after the baby was born and, though no one was smiling (that was not the practice of the day—after all picture taking was a very serious affair), everyone seemed to be enjoying good health. However, in a few years tragedy struck. When their son, Earl, was ten years old, his mother died giving birth to his baby sister, Ethel. Millie was only thirty years of age at her death.

Because of that turn of events Grandpa was a thirty-five year old widower with a ten year old son and an infant daughter to care for, plus a farm to run and a living to make. He struggled alone for a little over a year in that seemingly impossible situation. How he managed it we will probably never know, but the children and he survived. In all likelihood he was largely assisted by neighbors and some of his seven siblings, most of whom had settled on farms in that vicinity. His parents, James Hervey and Frances Maria, were both deceased. His mother died in 1872 at the age of thirty-five, and his father died in 1888 at the age of seventy, just four months before Grandpa Davis and Millie were married.

During the year of his struggle, Grandpa Davis became aware of a young, attractive neighbor girl, named Nettie Johnson, who attended the same one-room Hub School where his son, Earl, was a pupil. In a school photograph, taken in 1898, she is standing with the older students in the back row, while Earl is pictured with the younger students in the front row. Nettie's parents, Olive and Stephen Johnson, though they both look rather grim in their photographs, showed at least a smidgen of humor in naming their children. In descending order by age, they were Hettie, Nettie, Rettie, Lettie and Harvey. I have a photograph of the entire family, except for Lettie who died at a very young age. The picture was probably taken shortly before my grandmother and grandfather were married. It shows a very handsome family, with the real standout being Nettie, who is a statuesque beauty. William Davis and Nettie Johnson were married in 1901 and their wedding photo shows a gorgeous eighteen year old bride next to her handsome thirty-six year old groom. He was exactly twice her age!

I feel certain that theirs was a marriage of convenience. It surely was no match made in heaven as subsequent events bore out. They probably had little in common from the start. Being an entire generation apart in age was only one bump in the rocky road of marriage which they traveled. I'm certain that for Grandmother, having a step-son who was a mere seven years younger than she certainly didn't help either. She and her step-daughter, Ethel, who was only a year old at the time of their marriage, also did not hit it off well. Years later when I talked with both of them about the

4

relationship, each of them had a totally different assessment of it. Grandmother claimed that Ethel was disrespectful to her and that she was nasty and mean to the other six children that began arriving within a year. Ethel claimed that Grandmother mistreated her from the beginning and later favored her own children over Ethel. It was not a happy household.

Family photographs taken about 1906 and 1911 tell a little of the marriage story. In the 1906 picture William and Nettie have two additional children. Nettie is still slender, dark haired and very elegant and extremely attractive. William, however, who is forty, has begun to put on weight and his hair has started to gray and recede. From that picture one would assume that there were more than eighteen years separating them. The 1911 photograph continues the tale: By that date four of their eventual six children had been added to the mix. Nettie, then still only twenty-eight, looked fantastic. She peered out at the camera through clear eyes set in an unlined face. Her dark hair was arranged in an elegant upswept style. In contrast, William, then forty-six, who was holding my aunt Norma on his lap, appeared to be a short, fat elderly man. The hair was totally gone from the top of his head, and the little fringe remaining above his ears was nearly white. He had gained a great deal of the weight which would remain with him for the rest of his life. As an interesting sidelight, my dad, who died in 2002 at age ninety-four, appears in that picture as a four year old, leaning against his mother's knee and looking shyly at the camera.

My first recollections of my grandmother began about 1936 when I was four years old. Occasionally we would drive to their farm, which was located about five miles from ours, to visit. Grandmother Davis seemed just a bit forbidding to me when I was a child. She was very tall and somewhat severe looking. My distinct impression was that she rarely smiled and almost never laughed. Ever outspoken, she was very quick to reprimand her grandchildren if they had the audacity to break any of her rather stringent rules of behavior. My mother and she would, upon occasion, exchange sharp words over her punishment of us children. I feel that Grandmother Davis was very unhappy in her somewhat unusual marriage. She seemed to be much more cheerful and given to laughter and frivolity later during her years of widowhood.

Grandmother Davis's home was always immaculate. I do not recall things ever being out of their assigned place. Often the house would be redolent with her baking and cooking artistry. She was an extremely accomplished cook and an even better baker. During the summers her pies and cakes could be found cooling on the sill of the open window of the kitchen. When visiting, if the weather permitted, we would sit on the side porch that the kitchen window opened onto. Those aromas were most tantalizing to us. Invariably she had a filled cookie jar from which she would let us each take "just one!" Her sugar cookies and molasses cookies were mouthwateringly delicious.

At one point in their married life, Grandpa Davis owned a Model T two-door sedan. I'm not certain what happened to that auto, but it was gone before my first memories of visiting them. By that time their sons, Mickey and Maurice, were taking care of most of the couple's major transportation needs. But as far back as I can remember, whenever Grandmother wished to go into the town of Tuscola, roughly three miles away, she would walk. And, could she ever walk! She loved it! I still can picture her erect posture as she took those quick, long, strides. Because of her long legs, I could never keep up with her. She much preferred walking without Grandpa along because she complained that he was just too slow. By that time he was already in his seventies and looked as though he were at least ten years older than that, while she was a very young looking fifty-something. I have only one picture taken during those years which shows both of them together. Usually she refused to be near enough to him to be included in the same photograph. In that particular snapshot she towers over him by a minimum of six inches, and seems to be ignoring him as she is leaning away and looking off in the distance. She appears haughty and elegant. He is wearing his farm overalls and looks anything but elegant. At that point in their married life they were totally estranged from one another and soon parted ways completely.

To my four or five year old eyes, Grandpa Davis was ancient from the first time I became aware of him. He seemed much more intellectual and philosophical than Grandmother Davis. He read widely, but was particularly interested in history. One of his prized possessions was a twenty volume history of World War I, which was passed down to me at the time their household goods were dispersed among their heirs. I had earned a bachelor's degree in history at

Michigan State University and was teaching English and American history at Arthur Eddy Junior High School in Saginaw, Michigan at the time.

Grandpa Davis was something of an egoist and enjoyed being admired. He loved to tell tales about his youth. His memory was phenomenal. Though not particularly religious he could quote verbatim passage after passage from the Bible. That talent was especially impressive to me as I had serious problems with memorization. Politics was another favorite of Grandpa as a topic of conversation. At family get-togethers the entire Davis clan frequently erupted into shouting matches over different aspects of the politics of the day and Grandpa Davis loved to be a part of those heated debates.

Some time in 1941, my dad got a message that a family crisis was brewing at his parents' home. We didn't have a telephone as yet so I'm not quite sure how he learned about the problem. He drove to the Davis farm and found Grandpa staying out in the woods at the back of the acreage in the maple syrup shanty. That was a little building with a large trough where the sap from the maple trees was boiled down into syrup. Grandpa and Grandmother were refusing to speak to one another. He accused her of purposefully scalding him while applying a mustard plaster to his back. She, of course, denied it and declared, in no uncertain terms, that she would not have anything to do with him any longer. She insisted that some other living arrangements be made for him.

Dad brought Grandpa home with him and he stayed with us for a period of time. Relations in the, then, three generation household did not run smoothly and eventually, Mother and Dad moved him to a local nursing home. I recall visiting him there with my dad and hearing him beg and even cry to go home with us. That was a sad and moving experience for me as an eleven year old boy. My Uncle Clinton and Aunt Ellen offered to let him live with them, which he did during the short time he had remaining. He died in January of 1943 at the age of seventy-eight and was buried in the Davis plot in the Tuscola Cemetery. Grandpa, an avid history buff, surely would find it interesting that he was born during the Civil War and died during World War II.

At the time of Grandpa Davis's death, Grandmother was a very active and young fifty-nine year old lady with nearly twenty-four years of her life ahead of her. She lived alone for many of those years, took care of her house, cooked, baked delicious fruit pies, made patchwork quilts (one of which I still have), and walked to town regularly. My older brother tells me that she even took a job as a housekeeper for a family in the city of Flint for a short period of time.

Later Grandmother joined the Eastern Star organization, and became active in an association known as the Blue Star and Gold Star Mothers. Its members were women who had sons or daughters in the armed services. Her designation as a Gold Star Mother indicated that her son (my Uncle Mickey) had been killed in the war effort. He was in the U.S. Navy and died at the allied invasion of Normandy in France during June of 1944. The Blue Star and Gold Star Mothers did volunteer work at the various hospitals in Saginaw, a city twenty miles west of Tuscola.

In June of 1965, Grandmother became very ill. She was living alone at the time so she walked about a quarter of a mile to the farm of her nearest neighbors, the Coles. They called an ambulance and she was taken to Saginaw General Hospital (where she often had done volunteer work.) Grandmother was diagnosed with a perforated intestine and was placed on a life support system in the Intensive Care Unit. Apparently she contracted peritonitis and soon lapsed into a coma. Our family kept a day and night vigil during the two weeks that she lingered. She passed away on July seventh of that year, a little over two months before her eighty-third birthday.

Grandpa Davis and his first wife, Millie, rest side by side in the Davis plot in the local cemetery. But, Grandmother Davis had no intention of being interred near either of them, therefore, a few years before her death, she bought a group of cemetery lots well away from the Davis plot. That is where she lies today, next to a gravestone commemorating her son who died in World War II. Even in death Grandpa and Grandmother are a dysfunctional couple!

CHAPTER 2

THE JACK OF ALL TRADES

THE JACK OF ALL TRADES

Carpenter, photographer, casket maker, mechanic, laundry owner, furniture maker, blueprint reader in a streetcar factory, grocery store clerk, rug weaver and day laborer in a metal stamping factory—these are only some of the various occupations that my multi-talented Grandfather Williamson pursued during his working years. It always seemed that he could successfully do anything that he attempted, except earn a comfortable living for himself and his large family.

My mother's father, Jacob Franklin Williamson, usually called "Frank", was born in Findlay, a small city in northwestern Ohio, on May 30, 1867, just two years after the Civil War ended. He was the second child of Abraham and Almira Williamson. Frank's two sisters, Sophia and Minnie, both died before they were two years old. His older brother, Levi Marshall, the only one of his siblings who grew to adulthood, lived most of his life as a deaf mute, due to a childhood bout with scarlet fever contracted while the family was on a trip to Gagetown, Michigan to visit the children's grandfather. The family lived in Ohio until shortly after Levi was enrolled in the Michigan School for the Deaf in Flint, Michigan. To be nearer to him they moved to Vassar, a small town in Tuscola County, about thirty-five miles north of Flint. Abraham, worked as a carpenter in Vassar and died of consumption (tuberculosis) when the boys were twenty and fourteen respectively. Almira never remarried.

Frank was twenty-six in 1893 when he married seventeen year old Maude Dette Townsend. Maude was reared on a farm southwest of

Vassar. She was the second child of Sarah Jane and Carmel Townsend. A family photograph shows the three of them taken when Maude was a young girl of two. She is sitting on her handsome father's lap next to her rather plain mother. She is not a pretty child.

The Townsends had four children in all. The eldest, Winslow, died before his first birthday. The second was my grandmother and the third was Mabel whose August nineteenth birthday I share. She was exactly fifty-three years older than I. The youngest of the family was Joseph, who, at about the turn of the century, with a cousin and the cousin's wife, drove a horse and covered wagon, which he had built himself, to California and Oregon. He lived in Prineville, Oregon for the rest of his life and revisited Michigan only once during those years.

Joseph was still a baby at the time that his father, Carmel Townsend, committed suicide. Family lore tells us that Carmel felt he simply couldn't go on living after his wealthy mother, who lived near Akron, New York, disinherited him. She was upset with him for abandoning the rest of his family in New York and choosing to live far from them in remote Michigan.

The newly married Williamsons, Frank and Maude, set up housekeeping in Findlay and the first three of their eleven children were born there. By the time the fourth child appeared the family had moved back to Vassar, a move necessitated because Frank experienced difficulty making a living for his family in Ohio. During his early years in Michigan he pursued a wide variety of occupations, none of which seemed to provide him with enough income to support his family well.

In Ohio Grandpa Williamson had attempted unsuccessfully to earn a living as a photographer and continued that endeavor on a part time basis after the move to Michigan. Eventually he was able to purchase a photography shop from a man who was retiring. Grandpa went into business for himself and his eldest daughter, Mamie, worked for him. His studio was on the corner of Main Street and Huron Avenue above a drugstore in Vassar. In 1958, after I was graduated from Michigan State University and taught in the nearby town of Caro, I rented the apartment directly across the hall from that studio and lived there for about two years.

Though Grandpa Williamson was a talented photographer, he never made a real financial success of his studio. In the processing of his pictures he used glass negatives and I have a shoe box full of his negatives. After he died in 1941, somehow they ended up in my Aunt Lettie's barn. Everyone in the family had forgotten the negatives even existed until her death in 1985 when they were re-discovered. Then they were transferred to my cousin, Gene Seney, who stored them in his basement. They remained in that location until 1994. By that time I had become interested in the family's history. Gene's wife, Bonnie, passed the negatives on to me. Since then I have had most of them developed and the resulting photographs are a family treasure. Many of the negatives depict Grandpa's very photogenic daughters and other relatives so they make a good pictorial record of the family.

In addition to portraits of people, Grandpa Williamson photographed a number of scenic views in and around Vassar which he made into postcards and sold. I have a few copies of those postcards, and have seen many, many more in postcard collections. His scenic postcards are easily identifiable because he incorporated his trademark in the lower right corner of each of them. It consisted of his initials "JFW" printed by hand in his own distinctive way.

Grandpa Williamson later abandoned the photography business because of failing eyesight and took up his father's profession of carpentry and furniture making. For his woodworking artistry he used various hardwoods, like oak, maple and walnut. I have seen several chests of drawers which he designed and built. They are exquisite. The most distinctive thing about them was their drawer handles. He carved them out of solid wood into the shape of a cluster of acorns surrounded by a couple of leaves. Occasionally he finished the handles in a contrasting stain from the rest of the chest and the net result is a stunningly beautiful piece.

Among the other wooden items which Grandpa Williamson made were musical instruments such as mandolins and violins. I remember him building one particular violin that had a most unusual cover. It was constructed from many tiny pieces of various wood types and colors, none of which was larger than an inch square. They all were glued together to form the whole. When he showed the violin to me shortly after he finished, I was amazed at the intricacy and workmanship involved. It was the work of a real artist.

According to my older brother, Mother often told a story about Grandpa Williamson that well illustrated his mechanical genius. At one point in his life he either bought, or was presented with an automobile. However, there was one serious catch to the deal. The entire engine was disassembled and lying in many pieces inside the auto! Undismayed, Grandpa set to work putting the innumerable parts together to form an engine once again. When it was reassembled, he installed it in the auto and ended up with a vehicle which he could drive. It seemed as though no mechanical problem was beyond his scope.

Grandpa Williamson always was a very quiet and taciturn man. Never once did I ever hear him raise his voice. If he had strong opinions on any subject he did not let it be known. I can still picture him sitting in his favorite mission style wood rocking chair in a corner of the family's dining room smoking his pipe. He was a voracious reader and much preferred that to conversation. If someone brought up a controversial subject, he never rose to the bait to involve himself in either its defense or damnation. Instead he would become even quieter. Argument and debate simply were not his forte.

A large number of old family photos prove conclusively that my Grandmother Williamson was very homely. She epitomized two of the definitions of that word. The first definition is "homelike" and the second is "lacking in physical beauty." She had a big lantern jaw, a very heavy lower lip and a long, prominent nose which dominated the center of her face. In one photograph, where she is standing next to

Grandpa, she is wearing a wide-brimmed hat and looks exactly like the Wicked Witch of the West from "The Wizard of Oz"!

It wasn't until I was grown up and looked at Grandmother Williamson's pictures with a more critical eye, that I discovered she was physically unattractive. To my youthful eyes she was beautiful. Kindly and loving, she was the ideal of what a grandmother should be and she was far and away my favorite adult. Unlike others, she really listened to me when I had something to say and never ever "talked down" to me. Her lap was the most comfortable place to curl up in that I had found up to that time. Staying overnight at her house was one of my favorite activities. She was gravely ill during much of the time that I knew her, but that never kept her from being the doting grandmother she always had been. When she died in the fall of 1942 I was only ten years old and missed her terribly. Hers was the first funeral I ever attended.

Grandmother Williamson's long illness, though it was not the cause, probably contributed to a series of events that marked a very unhappy period for the family. In order that he would not disturb her, Grandpa stopped sharing the downstairs master bedroom with Grandmother and began sleeping in one of the upstairs bedrooms. The couple's youngest children, a boy about twenty and a girl in her teens, occupied the other bedrooms on that floor. At some point Grandpa began having sexual relations with his own daughter, and in 1934, when he was sixty-seven and she was eighteen, he impregnated her.

The daughter, a senior in high school, was coerced by the family to quit school and to stay in a home for unwed mothers near Detroit until she gave birth. The baby, a girl, was born shortly before her mother's nineteenth birthday and three months later she was adopted by a childless, older couple who lived on the east side of the state. The daughter returned to Vassar and completed high school a year late. In the 1930's having a baby "out of wedlock" was considered exceedingly shameful. Of course incest is something which even today isn't discussed in polite society. Therefore those events were kept very "hush hush" and only the immediate family knew anything about them at all.

My generation of the family didn't learn about the episode until many years later when the child became an adult and was about to be married. Her adopted mother placed an ad in the Vassar newspaper and was able to make contact with my aunt and invited her to the wedding. Later the daughter was introduced to the rest of the family. She and all of us cousins still didn't know who her birth father was. That was the state of affairs which remained for several decades.

One day in 1990 my aunt called and said she had something to discuss with me and asked me to come and see her. It was during that visit when she told me about the sordid affair and then asked if I would help write the entire story from <u>her</u> point of view. She felt that she had borne the sole blame for the pregnancy far too long. We wrote the story and later she sent copies of it to all of my cousins because she wanted them to know the truth. That action served as a catharsis for her and she felt that she had at last been vindicated. She died six years later, in 1996.

By the time the above mentioned events occurred, both Grandpa and Grandmother Williamson had been long in their graves. He died in June of 1941, a month before his seventy-fourth birthday, and she died in October of 1942 at the age of sixty-six.

There is an interesting and heartwarming side to this otherwise sad tale. My aunt's daughter, who is my half aunt and half cousin, has been a well loved part of our family from the time she became known to us. She fits in so well that it seems as though she has always been in the family. She and her children and grandchildren attend all the family functions and get-togethers and are wholly integrated into the clan. We feel very fortunate that she and they are a part of us. Our only regret is that we did not know her during the formative years when she lived with her adoptive parents.

CHAPTER 3

A HARD MAN
TO KNOW

A HARD MAN TO KNOW

By the year 1907, when my dad was born, the United States was beginning to flex its muscle in the worldwide political arena. That year Theodore Roosevelt was in the middle of his second term as President and in keeping with his diplomatic policy of "speak softly but carry a big stick" he decided to display the nation's might by sending the navy on a "good-will" tour around the world. The "Great White Fleet" as it was called, consisting of sixteen battleships and four destroyers, spent a total of fourteen months on the 46,000 mile "saber rattling" tour. President Roosevelt's action proved to the world that the country's naval power could move anywhere on the high seas quickly and easily.

Several hundred miles from the sea, on August twenty-eighth of that year, Dayton Wendell Davis was born on his father's farm. The farm was situated near the village of Tuscola, in the rural Michigan county with the same name. Dad was the third child of William and Nettie Davis and, in all, he had seven siblings. His father had been married and sired two children, Earl and Ethel, by his first wife before being widowed in 1899. A year later he married Nettie Johnson and together they had six children. From the eldest they were Leona, Maurice, Dayton, Norma, Clinton and Melvin (Mickey).

I have never heard my dad talk much about his early childhood, therefore, my information is sketchy at best. The farm on which the family lived was a mere eighty acres in size and provided the large Davis family with only a meager living during the best of times.

Much of the acreage was light sandy soil that produced only poor to average crops, and another section was devoted to a woodlot and Maple sugar grove.

The family worked very hard to wrest a living from the small farm. They raised a few row crops for sale on the open market and also produced the feed crops necessary for a small herd of dairy cattle and a flock of chickens.

While Dad was a child his family replaced the original farmhouse with a new one and later added on to the new house shortly after he left home to become a hired man on a neighboring farm. They nearly doubled the size of the barn during those years, too. They built a dairy stable against the rear wall of the barn that met the original structure at right angles. The addition was a few feet lower than the main part of the barn and the two floor levels were connected by a cement ramp. Years later, during visits to the farm, I enjoyed the childish excitement of running down that ramp into the dairy barn.

From the few things that he did say about his childhood, I gained the distinct impression that Dad's parents were extremely strict and, at times, cruel with him. One example of that cruelty is shown in the following story. He was given the responsibility of being in charge of the flock of chickens. He had to feed and water them, clean out the manure from their coop, see that they were bedded with clean straw, and gather the eggs that they produced. He related that at one point, for some unknown reason, the chickens began to lay fewer eggs. When my grandparents discovered the shortage, they gave Dad a whipping for allowing that to happen.

Little wonder that he left the home farm to work elsewhere as soon as he was old enough to do so. Dad got a job as a hired man on the George Hart farm which was located a few miles north and west of his parents' farm. Mr. Hart was a well-to-do dairy farmer who had no one to help with the work, so he was forced to hire the laborers he needed. Even though he was absent from the Davis farm that did not end Dad's responsibility there. According to the way my grandparents saw it, he should help out on their farm during weekends and any other time off from his job with the Harts. The Davis farmhouse was being added on to—in fact, it was nearly doubling in size—and he was expected to spend all his free time helping with the construction.

Down the road about a mile to the west from the Davis farm was the Hub School. It was a one-room country school where children from kindergarten through the eighth grade attended. Like his mother, Nettie, Dad went to school there until he had completed the eighth grade. I have a photograph of the Hub School taken about the year, 1917. It shows ten pupils (five boys and five girls) and their teacher standing in the front yard with the school as a backdrop. He, his sister, Norma, and his brother, Maurice, are all in the picture. The boys are dressed rather formally and sport suit jackets, knickers and knee socks.

After he was graduated from the eighth grade at the Hub School, Dad transferred to the Tuscola School, about two miles northeast of the Davis farm. At the Tuscola School, which I also attended from kindergarten until about the middle of the fifth grade, he completed the ninth and tenth grades, thus ending his formal education. I feel certain that if the Tuscola School had offered study beyond the tenth grade, he would have taken advantage of it. Vassar, five miles away, was the only area school that educated students through the twelfth grade. To complete those grades it would have been necessary for him to room and board in Vassar, and the money to do so was lacking.

I have Dad's Tenth Grade Diploma. It is printed on very heavy paper and is tied into a scroll with a fancy red ribbon with gold edges on which "Class of '23" is emblazoned. The heavily decorated and official-looking document states, "This Certifies that The Public High School of Tuscola Hereby Confers the Honor of Graduation upon Dayton W. Davis." It is signed by Archie E. Torrey, Superintendent of the school, and Howard E. Slafter and Robert Thompson, President and Secretary of the School Board, respectively. Rolled up inside the diploma is another certificate of honor for regular and punctual attendance. It indicates that Dad was neither absent nor tardy during the last year he was in school. He received the diploma and certificate of honor in May of 1923 when he was fifteen, three months before his sixteenth birthday.

My mother and Dad met during his trips to and from Vassar to pick up his younger sister, Norma. She was boarding at Mother's family home while attending high school in Vassar. By that time Dad had purchased a Model T Ford automobile and was happy and proud to show it off. Mother was one of six Williamson daughters. The eldest four, Mamie, Lulu, Lettie and Florence, had already married and were living elsewhere, but Mother and her younger brother, Bob, and sister, Marguerite, remained at home. Upon occasion the pair had run across one another in Tuscola, too. Mother's next older sister, Florence, had married Howard Baldwin and lived in that town. Mother and Dad both had been invited to get-togethers at their home.

The two young people began dating while Mother was a senior in high school. They were married about a year after her graduation when she was twenty and he was nearly twenty-two. Dad was then employed at a Chevrolet automobile assembly plant in Flint, Michigan, and, with some of his new-found wealth, had purchased a new gray Whippet auto with a "state of the art" self-starter. (No more cranking by hand for him, *he thought!*) Later developments were to prove him wrong, however.

For their honeymoon, the young pair chose to make a driving trip into the Upper Peninsula of Michigan to a scenic vacation area at Tahquamenon Falls in Chippewa County. *The Song of Hiawatha*, a poem by Henry Wadsworth Longfellow, was written about the upper and lower falls. That six hundred mile round trip was an impressive undertaking for a couple of relatively inexperienced young people in 1929. Most of the route went through very remote rural areas of the state. There were few paved roads, gas stations were miles apart, mechanical garages were practically nonexistent and restaurants and hotel or inn accommodations were in very short supply. Dad and Mother took along a tent and other camping supplies, plus most of the food that they would need during the trip.

According to both of them, they had a wonderful time. The weather was delightful and the scenery in upper Michigan was spectacular that summer. They made the first two hundred and twenty-five mile leg of the trip—as far as Mackinaw City—in good time with little difficulty. Mackinaw City is at the northern-most point of the Lower Peninsula of Michigan and is where one boarded the auto ferry for the Upper Peninsula town of St. Ignace. Today the impressive Mackinac Bridge connects the two peninsulas. At Mackinaw the pair enjoyed watching the shipping activity as the large, lake-going ships passed from Lake Huron on the east into Lake Michigan on the west and vice-versa. They had time to sight-see and take photos while they waited for their auto ferry to take them across to St. Ignace.

The ferry crossing was especially exciting for both as it was the first time that either of them had sailed on anything other than a rowboat in the river. At St. Ignace they spent the night before starting out on the last leg of the journey. Tahquamenon Falls is situated about eighty-five to a hundred miles northwest of St. Ignace through some of the wildest and roughest terrain in Michigan. Today the route follows well-paved roads with many tourist conveniences along the way, but that was not the case when they first made the journey in 1929. They finally arrived at their destination after several flat tires and other types of break-downs, and both of them felt that all it took to get there was well worth it. One of the pictures that Mother took made the falls look very much like a smaller version of the American side of Niagara Falls. That photograph, which they had framed, sat in an honored place on a table in our living room during my childhood. Their honeymoon lasted a week, at the end of which the couple came back to Tuscola and rented a small house there. They were ready to begin their married life in earnest.

In a short time Dad started negotiations to buy a small farm just north of Tuscola. He managed to scrape together enough money for the down payment, but had to borrow the major portion of its cost. They moved into the house on the farm within a few months after their marriage—shortly after learning that they were going to be parents. Six months later, my older brother, Laurel, nicknamed "Buddy", was born on June 25, 1930. Dad seemed delighted to have a son. Photo after photo shows the two of them together when Buddy was very young, and in each, the pride of fatherhood is clearly reflected in Dad's face.

I firmly believe that I was a real disappointment to my dad. He and Mother wanted their second child to be a girl, but I came along instead. I have no memories of him ever taking any time for bonding with me like he did when my brother, Buddy, was very young. I can find no pictures of him holding me or making any sort of fuss over me like in the photos of him and Buddy. My earliest memories of Dad's and my interaction are all negative in nature. He was the disciplinarian in the family and he frightened me badly. All too often I recall him using a heavy razor strop to paddle me, even though I would do nearly <u>anything</u> to avoid his wrath. In retrospect, it seems impossible that I was so fractious that such frequent and vicious punishment was called for.

My childish inability to swallow pills led to a very violent, and for me, traumatic confrontation with my dad. I have no idea why, but as a child, I never could swallow pills, either dry or with water. No matter how hard I tried, the pills invariably lodged somewhere under or beside my tongue. He thought that was a lot of foolishness and felt certain that he could solve the problem. First he <u>ordered</u> me to swallow them. I desperately attempted to obey, but the pills remained un-swallowed. Next he tried to force them down my throat by pushing them as far back as he could reach, and then holding my mouth closed. That didn't work either. I don't recall how the hideous session ended but I do know that I was completely traumatized and became even more frightened of Dad than I had been.

I have always had a strong aversion to blood. Often the mere <u>sight</u> of blood makes me nauseous and even causes me to faint upon occasion. I remember one episode between my dad and me where that aversion and weakness came into play. He always castrated all of the young male pigs that he was raising for slaughter. I was delegated to sit on the pig and hold its back legs while Dad performed the operation. During the grisly process, I became nauseated and inadvertently lost my hold on one of the pig's legs. The pig jerked and Dad cut himself with the sharp knife. He reprimanded me severely and indicated that he thought that I was some kind of a weakling for not being able to observe the operation with equanimity. The episode had one good result in that he never had me help with later castrations!

Little wonder that I was totally uninterested and even unwilling to learn to play softball when Dad wanted to teach me. He had played ball from a small child on and had always loved the game. Apparently he wanted to instill that same love in me. I wanted no part of him or softball and I ended up leaving our little training session in tears. To this day I still have a definite aversion to organized sports that I feel stems from my poor relationship with him.

Dad was always a very hard worker. During those early years, he spent about an hour and a half each working day in transit to the auto plant and his work there was physically exhausting. Every hour that he had free from the factory he labored on the farm. The Great Depression was in full swing during the 1930's and early 1940's so crop and milk prices were low and farm income suffered. The only way that our family was able to make it financially was because of Dad's job in the factory. Many farmers during those troubled years were forced into bankruptcy and had to abandon their agricultural operations.

Since he had to work so hard, Dad expected the rest of the family to do the same. He was the unquestioned "Boss" and all other members of the family were his underlings. Even Mother was expected to shoulder the burden of much of the farm work in addition to her many duties in the house. As very young children we were given chores to do after school and "woe unto us" if we failed to do them. From the time that we were ten years old, we were considered as laborers from early morning when we did the milking, throughout the day working in the fields and until the evening milking was finished. Only then did we have time to pursue our own interests.

Because Dad had only a tenth grade education and Mother was a high school graduate, he seemed to feel inadequate. He compensated for those feelings by adopting an air of superiority over her. He corrected her every statement. If she said that a room was ten feet long, he said it was twelve, if she said that an event occurred at noon, he said that it was at quarter 'til twelve. He corrected her no matter where they were or whom they were with. He took absolute delight in pointing up even the tiniest little discrepancy in anything that she said. Often he mortified her in public, and because he ruled supreme, she had little or no recourse. She accepted the embarrassment with the best grace possible under the circumstances.

After Dad sold the farm near Vassar, he worked for the Tuscola County Road Commission for about ten years. He retired from that job in 1972 when he reached the age of sixty-five. From that time on he and Mother spent much more time together and Dad became even more critical of her every move and statement. The problem grew to the point that I found it an embarrassment to be around them. It is difficult to break habits learned as a young child. From an early age, it had been ingrained in me that he was the one and only authority figure, so I was very hesitant to step in. In spite of my reluctance, I knew that something had to be done. I challenged him a few times in a polite way, and his reaction was explosive. He simply couldn't believe that someone had questioned his authority. His feelings were hurt! Later, he took his revenge, not on me, but on Mother! He claimed that she had caused the problem. Not even once did I ever hear him admit any guilt or any bad feelings over his verbal abuse of Mother. He felt that it was his right to do so—in fact, he never even recognized that he was being cruel at all!

Once when I challenged him about his abuse of Mother, he told me that it was none of my business and if I didn't like it I didn't have to come and see them. I responded that he wasn't going to keep me from visiting my mother. Then he very sarcastically asked, "Just what are you going to do about it?" My reply was that I was going to make different living arrangements for Mother if he refused to change his ways. Our confrontation that day did help, at least for a while. I later heard that he complained loudly and clearly to my brother, Buddy, about my "mistreatment" of him.

Though the last few paragraphs may make it sound as though I thought Dad was all bad, that is far from the truth. As Mother entered her eighties, she became much more infirm. She was bent over with agonizing osteoporosis and continually wracked with arthritic pain. She had a very weak stomach so she wasn't able to take any but the mildest of analgesics, so she suffered constantly. When she could no longer do the housework, Dad, who had not made a bed or vacuumed a floor in fifty years, took over. He even did a good job of it. He helped her with the cooking and became rather adept at that, too. He gave her his arm whenever she walked anywhere because she was very unsteady on her feet. He took her to the doctor when she needed to go, he oversaw her medications and, generally, took good care of her. For all of that I feel that Dad deserves much praise and commendation.

When Mother died at eighty-six in 1995, Dad grieved for her—as we all did. Even though a big burden of responsibility was lifted from his shoulders, he missed her terribly. It is interesting to note that his and my relationship became somewhat closer after Mother's death. That improvement, however, began slowly. He and I had never been able to converse well on a one-to-one basis. We simply had no interests in common and so had little or nothing to say to one another. The problem was serious enough so that for a few months after Mother died, each time before I would telephone him, I listed the subjects that we might talk about. I did that in order that we would have something to say. I began to drive him different places, too. We visited some of our relatives, we attended Memorial Day celebrations and other types of events in Vassar and eventually we started to enjoy one another's company.

After I retired from teaching, I became interested in our family genealogy. Dad was able to give me much information about his side of the family. I recall one time, shortly after Mother died, I was attempting to learn more about one of my great-great-grandmothers, Jane Rosencrants. A distant cousin had given me some information about her. I questioned him, and to my amazement, he was able to relate the names and relationships of everyone from that cousin back to great-great-grandmother Jane, and then back down to my generation in the correct order! His memory was phenomenal. He continually surprised me with his almost encyclopedic knowledge of our family. Many times, since I've begun writing this book, I have wished that Dad were able to answer questions. He would be an excellent source for information about a wide variety of subjects.

In January of 1997 when he was eighty-nine, Dad suffered a massive stroke. For the next five plus years he was a helpless invalid.

He could say only a very few words, he was unable to walk and he was incontinent. In addition, he had a serious swallowing problem, therefore he ate only pureed food—even his water had to be thickened. His swallowing difficulty was much different than mine was when I was a child. His was caused by the paralysis of some of his swallowing muscles, whereas mine, I'm certain, was psychological. Dad had to be mechanically hoisted out of bed to a wheelchair in order to go anywhere. He was a patient at the Gladwin Pines Nursing Home for nearly all of those last years. Most things that Dad attempted to communicate to us were difficult for us to understand, but one thing he made very clear, he wanted to die! I certainly didn't blame him at all. If I had been in the hopeless condition that he endured for such a long time, that too, would have been my fervent desire. His wish was granted on February 21, 2002. Dad was ninety-four and a half years of age at his death.

CHAPTER 4

A RENAISSANCE
WOMAN

Jerry R. Davis

A RENAISSANCE WOMAN

My mother, Ernestine Vere Williamson, was born in Vassar, Michigan on July 1, 1909. She was the ninth child of Frank and Maude Williamson. Family lore tells us that she was a twin, but that her twin sister never developed in her mother's womb beyond a certain point. If that is true then apparently the twin arrived at the same time as my mother, but never lived after coming into the world. I have always greeted that information, which was passed down through the family by word of mouth, with a bit of skepticism. It is the type of information that families are apt to bandy back and forth but has little or no basis in fact. It does, however, make the story of my mother's birth somewhat more interesting.

The Williamson's were in dire economic straits during their entire married life. Grandpa Frank had tried several different careers in Findlay, Ohio—where they spent the first few years of their marriage—and later in a couple of locations in Michigan. They finally ended up in Maude's hometown of Vassar. At different times Grandpa was, among other things, a store clerk, machine operator, laundry owner, photographer and furniture builder. Mother, during her lifetime, loved to write stories about her family. Invariably the stories of her childhood relate the desperate financial situation that the family endured. One of her often told tales describes the Williamson's cupboard and pocketbook both being completely empty one winter day and the near miracle which saved them. It seems that there was a huge snowstorm, and Grandpa Williamson walked through the piles of snow to the center of town where he ran across one of the downtown merchants. The man hailed Grandpa as "just the person I wanted to see" and asked him to go home to get his camera and photograph the huge snow piles at the front of his store. Grandpa Williamson did so with alacrity. He took several pictures of that store and many others in the downtown area before he was done shooting for the day. He went home and developed the film in his darkroom and later brought the resulting photographs to the store owners. They were pleased and paid him handsomely for the pictures. Mother related that the amount that he received was much more money than the family had seen for a long time. That and the additional money Grandpa earned from later photographs was enough to get them through the winter.

Mother was a rather shy girl who loved to read and to write. She always earned high grades in both scholarship and deportment. When she was seven years old and in the first grade; the Vassar School building, which housed all the grades from kindergarten through high school, burned to the ground. One of her stories tells of the problems which the fire created for the school officials and students alike while a new school building was being constructed. She described the chaotic scene that found her class meeting in the basement of the Baptist Church, others meeting in rooms above the downtown stores, and still others getting together anywhere in the village that vacant space could be found. Having taught in secondary schools myself for over thirty years, I can well imagine the resulting confusion. Mother weathered through, however, and despite the chaotic conditions, ended up loving school.

The combination of Mother's good grades in school and her shyness provides the impetus for the following story that I have heard Mother relate over and over again, much to my amusement. As Mother entered her senior year in the fall of 1927, it occurred to her that, because of her grade point average, she was destined to become either the valedictorian or salutatorian of her graduating class. The honor of being one of the top two students in her peer group appealed to her very much, but there was one aspect of the honor that frightened her nearly out of her wits. *The valedictorian and salutatorian both were required to give an address before the assembled group on graduation day!* That, Mother felt, she simply could not do. Merely reciting in front of any of her classes gave her palpitations, so the idea of speaking formally before a graduation day audience scared her so much that she was sure that she would faint dead away on the spot. To avoid the situation she was going to have to do something and time was of the essence!

Mother, purposefully, began to slack off in her studies. She knowingly placed a few wrong answers on quizzes and tests. She misspelled some words and used incorrect grammar on some of her essays. She told her teachers that she didn't know the answers to questions when called on in class. She didn't do poorly, but simply didn't produce the same type of schoolwork that she had in the past. Consequently, several of her grades dropped to "B's." Mother's teachers noticed the change, and when they questioned her, she did not admit the true reason for the drop in scholarship. That state of affairs continued for the balance of the school year and Mother's campaign was a success. She was graduated third in her class and smugly sat in the graduation day audience as Fleming Barbour gave the valedictory address and Wilma Land gave the salutatory address!

While my mother was attending high school, her family, always short of money, took a boarder into their crowded home. The new addition to the family was Norma Davis from the village of Tuscola. Norma, the same age as Mother, and very close to her grade in school, boarded with the Williamsons during those years because there was no school bus transportation at that time. She lived with the family, ate with them and for the most part was treated as any other family member. On weekends one of Norma's older brothers, Maurice or Dayton, drove from Tuscola to Vassar and gave her a ride home to spend a day or so with her family. The Davis brothers got to know the Williamson family on those weekly excursions to Vassar. Ernestine Williamson and Dayton Davis began dating one another about a year before Mother was graduated from high school. A year after she was graduated they were married, on July 4, 1929, in a small, private ceremony at the Williamson home in Vassar. Ernestine had just celebrated her twentieth birthday three days previously and Dayton was going to become twenty-two in about two months.

Mother and Dad's wedding picture shows the two of them standing side by side in the garden behind the Williamson home. Dad, who is wearing glasses, looks as though he thinks the situation requires a serious demeanor so no hint of a smile adorns his face. He is wearing a somewhat wrinkled suit that looks a bit too large for him. Mother is wearing a lacy dress, a single strand of pearls, and is carrying a large bouquet of roses, carnations and other assorted flowers. She looks as though she is biting her lip in an unsuccessful attempt to stifle a giggle. Though Mother is two years Dad's junior, she appears to be older than he. She has definite bags under her eyes and her skin doesn't have the smooth glow that twenty-year old skin usually has. The fault could be with the photograph because it is an enlargement of a small snapshot taken with an inexpensive camera. I don't know who the photographer was, as I found it among other photos in a box of pictures which Mother and Dad had for years.

For the first few months of their married life in 1929, Mother and Dad rented a small house in Tuscola. Dad was employed at a Chevrolet Automobile assembly plant in Flint and car-pooled the roughly seventy miles with several other men each day. Negotiations for buying their first farm must have been underway almost from the time of their wedding, because they moved into the house on that farm before my older brother, Buddy, was born in 1930, less than thirteen months after their nuptials.

Mother was a product of town life and must have found the farm existence to be far different from what she was used to. The farmhouse where she now lived was much like the house where she had grown up, because it lacked central heating, running water, insulation and even an indoor bathroom. But, she was not used to cows, bulls, draft horses, pigs, chickens and all the other things found on a farm. In a matter of a very short time, it was necessary for her to learn to feed and milk cows, clean stables, slop pigs, drive horses pulling farm implements, provide meals for large gangs of threshers, feed poultry, and even kill and pluck chickens. Those were things that a town-bred girl would hardly have been exposed to during her maturation. Dad was gone from the farm five or six days a week, and when he left she was fully in charge because there was no way for her to contact him. A few years after the farm was established Dad employed a hired man, but Mother still was saddled with the hour-to-hour decision making responsibility for the enterprise, in addition to seeing to the needs of four young children.

In one of her stories about her early married life, Mother talked about rescuing my older brother, Buddy, from a cow that had recently given birth and had turned vicious. It seems that Mother had set Buddy, who was at the crawling stage, down on the ground while she hung up the wash on an outside line in the yard. Momentarily unattended, Buddy crawled through the barnyard gate and was curiously looking at the angry cow as she snorted and pawed the earth in a threatening manner. Mother described how terrified of the animal she was. Somehow she managed to gather enough courage to reach through the fence and unceremoniously pull Buddy by one leg through the fence to safety.

During my lifetime I have known only two women whom I would judge to be truly self-educated. One of those was Maxene, my brother Buddy's wife, who had read all the classics of literature on her own and could hold forth intelligently on any subject. Conversationally, she far outdistanced most college graduates in my acquaintance and her knowledge of a wide variety of topics was almost encyclopedic. Besides my sister-in-law, Mother was the only other self-educated woman with whom I've had much contact.

In her flawless penmanship, Mother wrote fascinating letters to friends and relatives who lived any distance away. Those letters were interesting to read and were errorless. There were no crossed out words, strikeovers or any other indication that she did not put the text down correctly in the first attempt. When I was away from home; whether at MSU, in Germany as an exchangee or later as a soldier in South Carolina, I loved getting Mother's letters. They were warm and informative and made me feel that I was right there rather than miles away. One of the disappointments about which she often complained was that her correspondents didn't answer letters often enough. I feel that most of them were simply overwhelmed by how often and well Mother wrote. She definitely was a hard act to follow!

Mother's grammar was excellent. After I had completed several college English courses, she and I, for many years, made a game of attempting to catch one another in grammatical errors or mispronunciations. Not only was that fun but it was educational for both of us and, in our game-playing, we learned much about the language. Though I had taken many more advanced courses than she, her knowledge of grammar was equal to or better than mine. I never felt as though I was taking advantage of her lack of education and I feel certain that she didn't either.

In high school Mother had studied Latin for a couple of years. Most people who study that language in high school or college soon forget it completely. But, not Mother! All during her lifetime she was able to figure out or at least guess at the meanings of English words that had Latin derivations. I was amazed over and over again to listen to her while she verbally took an unfamiliar word apart into its basic parts and *Voila!*, in a few seconds she was able to give the approximate definition of the word. She was amazing!

Mother loved working with numbers. Each year during Income Tax preparation time she pored over the tax manuals for hours and hours. She taught herself to do the computations and complete the various forms for our farm Income Tax. In my opinion farm taxes are among the most intricate and mind boggling of all, so that was no small feat. Because of Mother's efforts, Dad never had to take the complicated mess to a professional tax preparer. Needless to say their farm taxes were never audited during all the years that Mother did the compilations. It was obvious even to the IRS that they were correct from the start!

I'm certain that I inherited my lifelong interest in home design and remodeling from my mother. When I was very young (probably five or six years of age) I remember seeing Mother making scale drawings of our farmhouse. She had entered a contest sponsored by *Better Homes & Gardens* magazine in which the contestants were asked to plan and illustrate the remodeling of their own homes. She ended up with pages and pages of "before" and "after" house plans, drawings of the remodeled house from all angles and even the planned landscaping around the house. She sent the collection to the magazine editors and impatiently awaited their response. After what seemed an eternity, she received a letter. She had won Honorable Mention and enclosed was a check for $50.00! She was ecstatic! Sad to say, but due to a shortage of money, the house never was remodeled while we lived there.

In 1964, when Mother and Dad sold the farm near Vassar, they retained a couple of acres just north of our old farmhouse. They built a new home on that piece of ground where our old pig lot had been situated. Mother designed and drew the plans for the new house from the basement to the roof and all that lay in between. It was a two bedroom home with a bath and a half, a fireplace between the living and dining areas, a wall of windows out of the back of the living room looking into the yard and garden, a double garage, a full basement and an in-the-wall central vacuum cleaner. The home was even heated electrically so no furnace was necessary. During the building of the house, Mother served as the construction supervisor, much to the irritation of the workmen. She and Dad were living next door in the old farmhouse so she was able to keep her eagle eye trained on them. Mother spent most of each workday at the new house and she caught the workmen each and every time they attempted to take building shortcuts. I feel that what irritated them most was that she actually knew what she was talking about!

Mother sewed most of her own clothing during her lifetime. She felt that store-bought clothes simply didn't fit her shape correctly and they were far too expensive. Her sewing machine turned out hundreds of items of apparel for herself, my sister, and even many of the shirts I wore when I attended Michigan State University. She knitted and crocheted a multitude of scarves, sweaters and many other useful goods. While listening to the radio, and later after the advent of television, her fingers were never idle during her favorite programs.

Her ability with a sewing machine qualified Mother for her first job outside the home and later led to her one and only business venture. Mother answered a help wanted ad in the Saginaw newspaper. An interior decorating business on the west side of the city was advertising for a seamstress who could operate the heavy-duty sewing machines making draperies and slipcovers. Mother applied for the position and was hired. She learned to measure, cut and stitch the material and became very adept at it. She worked for the decorating store for several years and then realized that she could do the same type of work without having to travel forty miles round trip each day. Mother opened her own business in our home, which she called "Davis Draperies". She successfully worked at the drapery and slipcover business for ten years or more. It was interesting for me to go into the different homes in and around Vassar and see examples of her handiwork at the windows and on the furniture. She even landed several good-sized drapery jobs for a number of corporate offices in Saginaw.

As Mother's age began to creep up, she was forced to limit herself physically, so she turned to less active pursuits. She became interested in genealogy and researched her own family line back about two hundred years. Later she did the same with my dad's family line. In the research process she wrote hundreds of letters and made family contacts that reached all over the United States. After her research and compilations were finished, she had me put all the information on the computer and make copies of both family trees for future generations. When I retired from teaching, I began assembling a collection of photographs of my direct ancestors, and, without Mother's genealogical research, that task would have been nearly impossible.

Mother became very frail and stooped during her eighties. She could get around by herself indoors, but needed Dad's assistance when going outside the house. She survived a hip replacement and a knee replacement fairly well, but was continually wracked with arthritic pain. She still read voraciously, wrote wonderful letters and cooked mouth-watering meals—though often with Dad's help.

In July of 1995, Mother fell and broke a hip for the second time. She was taken by ambulance to the Midland hospital about thirty-five miles from the little town of Gladwin where they were then living. Dad called me, and as I was driving to meet them at the hospital, I recall thinking that this setback probably would do her in. How right I was! She spent two miserable weeks in the hospital while they replaced her hip. Mother came through that operation all right, but shortly afterward other complications set in. At the end of her hospital stay she was moved to a nursing home in Midland. We visited her daily but she failed fast. She died on August 20, a little less than two months after her eighty-sixth birthday.

The following is an interesting anecdote about Mother's intellectual staying power. The day before she died, I was doing the daily crossword puzzle from the newspaper while sitting in her room. Mother was in and out of consciousness and I wasn't sure that she was aware that I was there at all. One of the crossword puzzle words stumped me and I read the definition out loud to myself. It was, "A long-grained type of Egyptian cotton." Mother heard me and said, "Pima." It was the correct answer!

CHAPTER 5

THE FOUR OF US

THE FOUR OF US

I have three siblings—my older brother, Laurel (Buddy to all of us), my sister Joanne, and my younger brother, Dan. It is obvious to me that ours was a planned family. Buddy was born just under twelve months after my parent's wedding, I came along slightly over two years later, Joanne was born just under two years after I was, and Dan, the caboose, arrived one month less than two years after Joanne. By the time Mother was twenty-six and Dad was twenty-eight, they were all through having children. I have known many couples that haven't even begun their families by those ages.

Buddy was the only person in our family with a nickname. Likely that was because he was the single one of the group, who was ever an "only child." He apparently was Dad's "Buddy", or pal from the moment of his birth. Family lore tells us that his official name, Laurel, was chosen by Mother because she had a distant cousin (called Aunt Mary) who lived in Hollywood, California next door to Stan Laurel, of "Laurel and Hardy" fame. Whether or not that story is true, his actual name is never used by anyone in our immediate family today. Grandmother Davis was the only relative who called him Laurel. One of her neighbors, whom she felt was a real reprobate, was nicknamed Bud. Grandmother declared that she would never call an innocent grandchild of hers by the same name as that despised neighbor. So she never did.

To me, Buddy was always my "big brother." I looked up to him with the admiring eyes of a child who was two years his junior (an eon at that age). He was more mature, more knowledgeable, stronger and much less excitable than I was. I recall going to him many times to have him explain a plethora of mysterious things about the adult world in which I found myself. Buddy rarely, if ever, let me down by not knowing the answers to my questions.

Unlike me, Buddy seemed to be fearless. I was afraid of many things, but especially of my dad who was the disciplinarian in the family. To me, he was a martinet. Buddy displayed absolutely no trepidation and challenged his authority with impunity. I recall seeing them rolling around on the kitchen floor fighting over his defiance of Dad's normally unquestioned commands. To me Buddy's challenge was akin to questioning God's power! I only <u>dreamed</u> of following suit, but was never able to put it into practice until nearly fifty years later.

Buddy had two consuming passions when he was a child. The first of those was for growing plants. He and my mother's eldest sister, Aunt Mamie, always had a lot to talk about when they got together as they both were plant enthusiasts. I'm certain that Buddy knew more about the nature and nurture of growing things when he was ten years old than I know today. His yard in Federal Way, Washington has examples of plants from all over the world that he has collected in his travels. He brings them back and invariably they grow and flourish under his tender loving care. He is very active, too, in the Master Gardener program for the Greater Seattle area.

Buddy's second passion, as a child, was for automobiles. He filled scrapbooks with pictures that he had cut out of magazines. He was able to name every American-made car and tell its year of production, and probably could do the same for most of the foreign-made autos, too. Later he was graduated from General Motors Technical Institute in Flint, Michigan with a bachelor's degree in automotive engineering. He was employed at GM for a number of years before accepting a position with Boeing Aircraft in Seattle, Washington.

My mother confessed to a close friend of mine, that when I was born, she and Dad were very disappointed because they both wanted a girl. In fact, she said because of that disappointment, she sometimes even dressed me in girl's clothing when I was a baby. Of course I have no memory of that and only learned of it when I was an adult. As far as I knew, my welcome into the family was as warm and sincere as Buddy's had been two years previously. My early childhood was happy; I had few responsibilities and enjoyed playing around the farmyard. I liked the animals—especially the horses with their soft, velvety muzzles and the baby calves with their large, brown eyes and rough tongues.

It wasn't until later, after I had to work on the farm, that I discovered how badly misplaced I was by being born to an agricultural family. As a farmer, my sympathies usually ended up in the wrong places. I felt sorry for the young pigs when they were being castrated, rather than feeling happy that later they would provide meat for our table. I grieved for the older horses when they were sold to the fertilizer plant to be ground up for plant food, rather than thinking how much better the farm work could be done with the new, younger team that Dad bought. Those two thousand pound creatures had been like giant pets to me. I held my ears so as not to hear the screaming and ran to the far side of the farm on pig butchering day, instead of thinking about how good the pork chops, loins, and sausages would taste. I had trouble watching a cow give birth because the sight of blood made me nauseous and feel like fainting, instead of rejoicing that the new calf would eventually provide more milk for sale and bring in needed money. I hated the fact that our living depended so much on the erratic vagaries of weather. I have seen my dad break down and cry when a heavy rain and wind storm flattened a wheat crop so badly that it couldn't be harvested and had to be plowed under. Yes, I was misplaced on the farm and yearned for the day when I could leave it permanently for other pursuits.

My childhood interests were predominantly in two areas, both having to do with drawing. I enjoyed depicting people, particularly ladies, and drawing the designs for their clothing. I'm certain that I bored many of our relatives and other guests by insisting that they look at every one of the drawings in my portfolio. To this day, I continue to be interested in drawing and sketching and enjoyed illustrating this book.

My second overwhelming interest as a child was in drawing houses and house plans. That was a passion that my Mother and I shared and we spent many fascinating hours comparing notes on house designs and floor plans, and more specifically, on the remodeling and restoration of houses. That interest led me to one of my summer jobs while I was in college. During that summer, I was employed at the Reindel and Bronner Lumber Company in

Frankenmuth, Michigan, and part of my time was spent in their Home Planning Department. In the three months that I worked there, I designed and drew plans for one remodeling and two entire homes, all of which eventually were completed.

My avid interest in houses and remodeling has remained with me all my life. Shortly before I retired from teaching junior high school, I began to buy old "junked" houses and devoted about a year each to restoring them and later renting them to tenants. By the time of my move to the Southwest, I had six houses in total. Not wanting to be an absentee-landlord, I sold all of them prior to leaving Michigan.

In high school I developed a third interest that lasted for a long period of time. I tried out for both the junior and senior plays, and to my surprise, earned roles in both of them! Later, when I was in the military service, I acted in several productions at Ft. Jackson, my army base, near Columbia, South Carolina. Upon my discharge, I immediately joined the Pit and Balcony Players in Saginaw, Michigan, and appeared in about a dozen shows for them and a couple for the nearby Bay City Players. In addition, I spent parts of two summers acting for the Sister Lakes Theatre, a summer stock company near Benton Harbor, Michigan. Since growing older, my interest in theater remains strong, but more as a spectator, than as a performer.

About twenty-two months after I was born, Mother and Dad's wish for a baby girl was granted when my sister, Joanne, joined the growing family. I don't remember her when she was very young, but Joanne's baby pictures show a happy, fat-cheeked infant girl who always seemed to be smiling, grinning or outright laughing. My first definite memory of her was in 1938 when I was six years old and she was four. Joanne and I were chosen to be in my Aunt Marguerite's wedding as flower girl and ring-bearer. A picture I have of the two of us at the ceremony, shows Joanne in her fancy new dress, with lots of ruffles, holding the bride's bouquet and laughing wildly, with her pudgy cheeks clearly evident. Apparently I thought that it was a rather more serious affair, so I only have a slight smile on my face. After all, I was two years older and much more sophisticated!

With Joanne being the only girl in the family, she was, by turns, coddled and protected by us boys, and on the other hand, teased unmercifully about nearly everything. I don't know how she felt about being the sole female among three boys, but I think she weathered it successfully, and in fact, held her own extremely well. In spite of Joanne's predominately male environment, she could never have been accused of being a tomboy. Apparently taking the lead of her two older brothers, she, too, was always shy in her dealings with most people outside our small family circle.

During high school, while enrolled in home economics courses and working with the 4-H Clubs, Joanne developed an interest in sewing. She became very proficient with a needle and thread and the sewing machine—she even made most of her own clothing. Later, Joanne and her husband, Richard, owned and ran a wood handicraft business for many years. Richard fashioned the items and she applied the finishes and decorated them. They displayed their merchandise at shows all around Michigan and in some of the neighboring states. Recently, they relinquished the business for health reasons.

For the last five years of Dad's life, Joanne and Richard had the sole responsibility for taking care of his affairs and seeing to his day-to-day needs. He was completely helpless in a nursing home about twenty-five miles from where they lived. They shouldered the burden willingly and did a very commendable job of it. All three of us brothers live hundreds of miles away in other states and we feel a real sense of gratitude that they were there for Dad and willing to do all the things that needed doing for his welfare.

My younger brother, Dan, joined the family in 1936. Like the three older children, he, too, was born in our farmhouse near Tuscola. I remember that afternoon very well, because he wailed loudly enough so that he could be heard throughout the entire household. He did not sound very happy about coming into the world! He may have been unhappy about being born, but the rest of us were delighted to have a new baby in the family. I was so young when my sister was born that I have no memory of her as a baby, but not so with Dan. I was four years old and was deemed old enough to actually hold him upon occasion. I recall being warned sternly about protecting his tiny head because a newborn baby's skull is very fragile.

Shortly after Mother weaned Dan from nursing, he developed a strong reaction to the formula that he was being fed. He simply could not hold it down. He threw up incessantly and was ill all of the time. Upset and frustrated, Mother took the suffering baby to Dr. Swanson, the family doctor, and learned that his stomach was unable to tolerate cow's milk. The doctor's recommendation was that he be fed goat's milk, which she tried. Dan was able to keep that smelly stuff down and began to thrive on it. He seemed to like the goat's milk. I thought that it was nothing but disgusting! Apparently Dan outgrew his bad reaction to cow's milk because he drank it regularly during his childhood, once he was beyond the baby stage.

Of the four children in our family, Dan was, by far, the most outgoing and gregarious. He was an excellent scholar, was active in sports, he excelled in music and was very popular with the teachers, his fellow students and his classmates. I recall seeing his picture in the high school yearbook the year he was graduated and being very impressed with the large paragraph of accomplishments that appeared below it. If there <u>had</u> been a yearbook the year that I was graduated, there would have been only two entries below my picture: the Junior Play and the Senior Play.

Dan went on to earn a bachelor's degree, a master's degree and a doctorate in business. For most of his career he taught graduate level university courses in business to servicemen in various European countries and several places in the United States and Cuba. He and his wife retired a couple of years ago and now do volunteer work in Florida.

My three siblings and I all left the farm years ago to follow other professions. I'm not certain how the others feel, but I think that I have had a most fulfilling and interesting life, and look forward to enjoying many more years to come. The four of us chose not to embrace agriculture as our careers. In spite of that fact, growing up on a farm helped us become well-grounded in many aspects of life which were applicable as well to other fields of endeavor. I'm certain that our rural childhood helped us learn self-reliance, the value of hard work, and the importance of helping our fellow man. Though as a child I thought that much of my work on the farm was boring, distasteful or downright demeaning, I persevered and survived and likely am a better man today for having done so.

CHAPTER 6

THE HIRED HELP

THE HIRED HELP

Many Michigan farm operations, both large and small, during the 1930's and even the 1940's employed a hired man who lived on the farm. He helped with all of the barn and field work, ate his meals with the farm family and in some cases became almost like a member of the family. One of our hired men, Jake Eichman, and his wife and children remained close friends with my family for forty or fifty years—in fact until his death.

In certain instances hired men only worked on a farm seasonally—during the spring planting or the busy harvest time. Large groups of Latinos from Mexico hired themselves out to Michigan farmers for temporary work hoeing beans, thinning beets or other types of work with crops that gave them employment for much of the summer. They didn't live with the family; instead they were provided very simple and often substandard housing elsewhere on the farm or in the neighborhood. The Latinos spent their winters in the southern states where they found other seasonal farm work.

My dad worked for a time as a hired man. He was employed by a Mr. George Hart who lived several miles north and west of Tuscola. Mr. Hart was a wealthy farmer with some of the best farm buildings in the county. He owned a large acreage with fertile soil and raised some cash crops but most of his income came from his large dairy herd. Mr. Hart's only son was physically unable to do farm work. Dad lived with the family and worked on their farm for a couple of years after he finished the tenth grade and left school. That was the highest grade offered in the Tuscola School. If Dad were going to go further he would have had to attend Vassar school which was about eight miles away from his father's farm.

The first farm that my dad owned, which he bought in 1930, was just north of Tuscola. He was unable to pay cash so was forced to borrow most of the purchase price. In order to keep the farm running and make the loan payments it was necessary for Dad to have additional income other than what the farm could provide. Therefore he kept his job at a Chevrolet automobile assembly plant in Flint, about thirty-five miles south of Tuscola. He had joined a car pool with several other men in the area and they made the sixty mile round trip daily. Because Dad was gone from the farm so much of the time, it was necessary for him to employ a hired man to do much of the heavy work.

I have no personal recollection of this, but my older brother tells me that the first man that Dad hired was his own uncle. My grandfather's younger brother, Wesley Davis, came to live with the family on the farm and helped out wherever he could. Great Uncle Wes probably was in his middle to late sixties at the time. I'm not at all certain how long the arrangement lasted or what caused it to come to an end, but I feel sure that it was of fairly short duration.

The first of our hired men whom I remember was a young fellow named Austin Stillwell. He was almost like a member of the family right from the start. We children particularly enjoyed him because he was a great story teller. He knew the Hans Christian Anderson fairy tales and many other stories which he loved to relate in his own entertaining way. Austin owned an automobile which I found fascinating. It was the first car I had ever seen that had a rumble seat. The seat was situated in the trunk's usual location. There was a door at the rear of the coupe which, when opened, would form the back of the seat. People sat there facing the front of the car and it was like riding in a convertible with the top down. When the door was shut it merely looked like a closed trunk. Austin was well liked by the ladies too. During part of the time that he was our hired man he dated my mother's younger sister, Aunt Marguerite. Years later, long after Austin had disappeared from the scene, my aunt told me she seriously regretted that they had parted ways and had never gotten serious about one another.

Austin worked on our farm for a couple of years and, when he left for other employment, he was replaced by a man named George Wilson. I don't remember very much about George—he obviously didn't make quite the deep impression on me that his predecessor did. I recall that he was very quiet and that he had a girlfriend. I remember the latter because she, too, worked for us. So, for a short period of time, we had both a hired man and a hired girl. George's lady friend, whose name I don't recall, worked for our family during part of the time when my mother was pregnant with my younger brother, Dan. One of the hired girl's assigned tasks was to do our family's ironing. For some strange reason I clearly remember her going out to the orchard just south of the house, picking several apples and then eating them while she ironed. Perhaps the reason that I recall the incident so well is that my mother complained that the girl did more apple eating than ironing!

None of our hired men lasted for a very long time. The pay was minimal, the hours were long and the work was hard, so after a time they looked for easier and more profitable jobs elsewhere. Working as a hired man usually was their first job as an adult. It served as a sort of springboard for them to leave home and be at least somewhat on their own financially. The Great Depression of the 1930's was in full swing until World War II began in 1941 so high paying jobs were rather scarce for young men without specialized training and marketable skills. The only real requirements needed for working as a hired man on a farm were average intelligence and strong muscles.

Jake Eichman followed George as our family's next hired man. Jake was a gregarious and hard working young man who loved excitement. He particularly enjoyed driving the team of horses and putting them through their paces. In fact, a number of times he, in his over-exuberance, accidentally allowed the horses to get away from him. A runaway team can be a danger to themselves, the equipment to which they are hitched, the person attempting to bring them under control, and anyone in the vicinity. Jake learned the hard way that driving a team of horses, each of which weighs nearly two thousand pounds, was very serious business, indeed. Luckily nothing tragic happened due to his carelessness while he worked on our farm.

Jake married his long-time girlfriend, Clara, shortly after leaving our employ. He took a factory job in Bay City and the couple built a house in Auburn a few miles to the west of where he worked. Jake

63

and Clara raised three sons in the house and lived there until he retired from the factory and moved to a Midland senior citizen apartment complex. Our two families visited back and forth often during the years that Jake and Clara were raising their children. I remember spending many Christmas and Thanksgiving celebrations with them. Jake told us that because his parents died when he was so young, he thought of my mother and dad as substitute parents for him and substitute grandparents for his children.

The last of our full-time hired men was a young lad named Charley. The last names of the other hired men came to me easily, but Charley's did not. Because I drew a total blank, my brother, Buddy, had to remind me of his, which was Wineman. Charley was very young and must have been rather incompetent at best. I know that my dad and mother complained bitterly about him. Needless to say he didn't last very long. By that time my dad no longer was working in the Chevrolet plant in Flint and was farming full time. He had sold the farm near Tuscola and we had moved to a much larger one just north of Vassar. My brother was twelve and I was ten and we were deemed old enough to be farmhands, so a hired man was no longer necessary in Dad's opinion.

Another man lived on our farm for a while after the last of the hired men left. His name was Ed Berg. He was an elderly gentleman who appeared at our door one day and just seemed to stay. He lived with us, helped with the care of the chickens and pigs, and assisted my mother in the garden. I doubt that he received much in the way of pay, other than his keep, but that seemed to be satisfactory with him.

He was an interesting old character and often smoked a pipe. I thought that the pipe had a really good smell, but my mother disagreed. One day when Ed was sitting in our kitchen next to the wood-burning range, I made a pencil drawing of him. It showed him with what looked like a week's growth of beard and his glasses resting half way down his nose while he smoked his pipe. The drawing really did look like him and both he and I were very proud of my masterpiece. He even showed it to some of his friends. Where Ed went when he left our farm, I have no idea.

I, too, served as a hired man on a farm for a short period of time. I was only sixteen when I was graduated from high school and began my first year at Michigan State that fall only one month after my seventeenth birthday. After completing my freshman year I was still only seventeen which was too young to get a good paying factory job. As I was working my own way through college I needed money, so I went to work for the Albert Bauer family near Reese. Their farm was about eight miles from ours and it was a large operation where they always needed help. The pay was rather low, but the Bauers provided for all my needs except clothing, so I was able to put most of my wages into savings.

My decision not to be a farmer was made years before the time I spent as a hired man working for the Bauer family. That type of work held no interest for me whatsoever. In fact, one of my main reasons for attending college was to get the training necessary to follow some career other than farming. I, like all the hired men that we had employed on our farm, used that job as a springboard to help me embark on a career which was much more to my liking. In my case that field of endeavor turned out to be teaching history in secondary schools.

CHAPTER 7

GOOD NEIGHBOR POLICY

GOOD NEIGHBOR POLICY

The neighbors whom I enjoyed best when we lived near Tuscola, on the farm where I was born, were the Wehrmans. They rented the place across the road and just south of our farm. The family consisted of Mr. and Mrs. Wehrman and their son, Reuben. As I remember they had another son named Carl, however he lived on the farm with them only a short time. In addition they had a married daughter who lived about ten miles away near the village of Reese. The daughter, Ruth Ahrens, and her family occasionally visited the Wehrmans and I got to know them and Geraldine, the granddaughter. Geraldine was about my age and we enjoyed one another's company and became good friends. In fact, I still call her upon occasion. Geraldine's husband, Lavern, died in August of 2000. She now winters in Florida and summers in Michigan.

When the Wehrmans moved to the farm, Mr. Wehrman was already retired and in very poor health. He died a short while later so I never really got to know him. I remember him only as an impassive figure sitting quietly in a chair in the yard during the warm seasons of the year and occupying a rocking chair before the kitchen range during the winter. Because he was so quiet, sometimes I even wondered if he were able to speak at all!

My favorite in the family, other than Geraldine, was Mrs. Wehrman. She was tall and slender, and, though she was in her mid fifties at the time, her hair showed no gray whatsoever. She laughed a lot and had the most interesting German accent I had ever heard. She had a delightfully warm personality and always seemed truly interested in anything I had to say. I passed their house daily as I walked to and from school and often stopped in to visit with her in the afternoon on my way home. Invariably she greeted me in a friendly way and the two of us always seemed to have a lot of things to talk about in spite of our age difference. Once in a while she offered me a cookie, which I, of course, accepted with pleasure. Mrs. Wehrman would question me about what was happening in our family, what I was doing in school and about how things were going on our farm. She would regale me with tales of what was going on in her family's life in a most entertaining way. We would laugh and talk for a half hour or so and then I would be on my way across the road toward home.

Reuben Wehrman, who was probably about thirty years old at the time, was the farmer in the family. He had total charge of the entire agricultural operation and seemed to take to it naturally. Once in a while he would come in the house to have a cup of coffee when I was visiting and he would join our little "chat session". He, like his mother, was a sincere and likeable person who truly listened to what I had to say and treated me as an equal even though I was many years his junior. He and my dad were about the same age and they became good friends and neighbored back and forth between the two farms. They helped one another on threshing day and corn husking day and were always there for one another when any kind of help was needed.

In 1942 we moved to the farm near Vassar but that didn't end the friendship between our family and the Wehrmans. We continued to see one another upon occasion. A few years later Reuben and his mother moved to a rental farm a mile or so south of the village of Millington about seven or eight miles southeast of Tuscola, but our two families still continued the relationship.

The last time I visited Mrs.Wehrman and Reuben was a few months before her one hundredth birthday. Though somewhat frail, she still was the same interesting and vital person she had been nearly fifty years before. She and I had an interesting time reliving the past and reminiscing about my after-school visits to their home. Her memory was as sharp as ever. She died when she was one hundred and one and my mother, my dad and I attended her funeral. Because she had lived so long, it seemed as though an institution had passed away. At the funeral I talked with Mrs. Wehrman's daughter, Ruth, her son, Reuben, and with her granddaughter, Geraldine. Geraldine was about to become a grandmother herself at that time. Reuben Wehrman didn't have the same longevity as his mother—we all met at his funeral only a short four years later when he was eighty.

My favorite neighbors when we resided near Vassar were the Saffords. They lived on the farm adjoining ours to the north. Evart Safford and his wife, Nellie, had raised three children, a son and two daughters, on that farm. One daughter and her family lived in Caro, a village about 15 miles to the northeast from Vassar. Another daughter lived with her family in Vassar. The third child, a son named Carl, and his family had an apartment in Flint—about thirty-five miles south of Vassar. He taught mathematics at a junior high school in that city.

Evart and Nellie Safford were good neighbors from the time we moved next door to them. Nellie (always referred to as "Mrs. Safford" by my family) was a dignified, gracious and grandmotherly lady. She was a wonderful cook who produced delicious meals for all of us neighbors when we came to help out on threshing day. The house had been built in 1930 and was very modern when compared with ours. It was a one and a half story Craftsman style house containing living room, dining room, kitchen, bathroom and five bedrooms, plus a full basement. Mrs. Safford was a good housekeeper and maintained the house in good order. She was a quiet and reserved lady who never found any reason for boisterous or rowdy activity.

Mr. Safford (we never called him that, instead he was always "Evart") was very different from his wife. Apparently it is true that opposites attract. He was a short, heavy-set, jolly man with one of the wildest senses of humor that I have ever encountered. I could listen to him for hours at a time as he regaled me with hair-raising episodes about his childhood and youth. I think that he purposely set out to titilate me with his ribald tales. The stories never shocked me, but they surely did provide me with no end of fascination. I envied him his happy and relatively carefree childhood which, I felt, was so different from my own. I felt sorry for myself because I had to get up early to milk the cows seven days a week, feed chickens, slop pigs and toil like a farmhand all the time I wasn't in school. To me my lot in life was bleak at best.

Because Evart had no children at home to help him with the farm work, he often would get permission from my dad for me to help him.

I loved it when that happened. He was a real pleasure to work for and with. Work that I would grumble about doing on our farm, I would happily do on his. His sense of humor and conversation made even the most laborious task a real joy. I used to daydream about being adopted by the Saffords and living there permanently. To my way of thinking, at the time, that would have been pure heaven.

In the summer of 1948 when I was fifteen, Evart provided me with the opportunity for my first business venture away from our home farm. He had an alfalfa field situated just south of the farmhouse that he didn't need for roughage for the Hereford steers that he was raising that year. He made me a proposition. He said that he would sell me the crop for $50.00 and it would be my responsibility to cut the hay, bale it and store it until I could sell the bales. Well, that was too good a proposition to turn down, so I paid him the money before he changed his mind. As it turned out, before I was ready to cut the hay, another neighbor, Ted Proffer, approached Evart and asked to buy the hay crop on that same field. Evart told him he was too late as the crop already belonged to me. Mr. Proffer came to me and made me a further proposition. He said that he would cut and bale the hay and then we could split the bales between us. That sounded good enough to me so I agreed. For my $50.00 cash outlay, and little or no work, I ended up with over a hundred bales of hay which I later sold for a dollar each—thus more than doubling my investment! Evart was delighted over my business acumen and enjoyed telling the story to others. Needless to say, I too was delighted.

I was graduated from high school a year later in 1949 and entered Michigan State University that fall. Because I was eighty-five miles away in East Lansing and busy with my college courses, I didn't see much of the Saffords during that year, but they were often in my mind. That next spring I received a telephone call at my dormitory from my mother telling me that Evart had died in his sleep—probably from a heart attack. I was stunned! He was closer to me than either of my grandfathers had been and I felt his loss much more than theirs. Because I had very few close friends of any age, the loss of one of them created a huge void.

Evart's son, Carl, his wife, Beth, and their three children, Ross, Carrie and Richard, soon moved to the farm to be with Mrs. Safford and help her manage the place. I continued to visit the farm and, even though I liked them and enjoyed being around the younger family, it simply didn't seem quite the same without Evart there. For a period of time, however, I did have one tangible bit of Evart memorabilia. Carl agreed to sell me his dad's black 1949 Ford automobile for $1,100. That was my first car. During the entire time I owned it, I often thought about the auto's former owner and relived the joy I had experienced listening to his wild tales. For me he lived on in that Ford car!

Carl's widow, Beth, still lives on the farm. Though she has had some bouts with ill health, I believe she lives alone. The farm is rather different than it was. One of the barns was torn down a few years ago, a stable and horse paddock were built back of the house where the garage used to be and the home has undergone a thorough remodeling. It has changed a great deal, but is still recognizable as the house I visited over fifty years ago. Evart's grandchildren now are adults with children and grandchildren of their own. Carrie and Richard both live in Vassar and Ross lives in Ohio. I write to Carrie once in a while and usually try to visit her when I make my yearly trip to Michigan. Thus my friendship with the Saffords continues to the present.

Though we didn't do very much in the way of pure socializing with our neighbors when I was growing up on the farm, nonetheless, they were extremely important to us. We interacted in ways that helped one another—such as communal threshing days, lending a helping hand when workers were not readily available and, in short, just being good neighbors. Our socialization took the form of mutual cooperation.

CHAPTER 8

TWENTY FOR LUNCH

TWENTY FOR LUNCH

Prior to the invention of the grain combine, which both cuts and threshes the grain in the field in one operation, the harvesting process was much more complicated. After the grain was ripe, the farmers first used a machine called a binder. During that procedure the grain was cut and tied into bundles, or *sheaves*. Then the farmer formed the bundles into stacks or *shocks* of about ten bundles each. He arranged them so that rainwater drained off, leaving the grain dry. In addition, having the bundles gathered into stacks made loading them on wagons more efficient on threshing day than if they were scattered across the field. When the grain was stacked, the farmer was finished with as much of the harvesting process as he could do by himself. He then had to wait for the arrival of the threshing machine.

The threshers were large, cumbersome and expensive machines not readily affordable to each farmer. In fact, the machine owners sometimes were not farmers at all. They owned the equipment and earned their livings by threshing for all the farms in the area and were paid a certain amount for every bushel of grain that was processed. Because the fields of wheat, oats and other grains in a neighborhood all ripened at approximately the same time, it was necessary for the machine owner to set up a schedule of threshing days for those farmers who were his customers.

Threshing day was a momentous event for the entire farm family. The thresher, pulled by a steam engine or other type of large tractor, arrived early in the morning, in order that the operator had time enough to go through the complicated set-up process. He had to grease and oil the machinery at the start of each day and make certain that it was in good operating condition. Breakdowns were costly and wasted precious time for everyone involved. The operator situated the thresher where it was easily accessible to the wagon loads of grain bundles that would soon arrive. He attached it with a thirty foot belt to the power source (usually the steam engine or tractor that had hauled it to the farm). He arranged the long pipe through which the straw passed so that the straw pile ended up where the farm owner wanted it. At the side of the thresher was another somewhat smaller pipe which had a cutoff lever. The kernels of grain, after being separated from the straw, came down that pipe into bags attached at the end. The cutoff lever allowed the man controlling that part of the operation to stop the flow long enough to attach an empty bag after the previous one had filled. When everything was in order, the operator usually ran a few trial bundles of grain through the thresher in order to ascertain that the equipment was working properly.

By that time the neighbors had arrived—each with a horse or tractor drawn farm wagon. Threshing day was a communal operation which required each farmer to assist his neighbors and, in turn, be assisted by them when his threshing day came. The wagons, which had open sides and a high rack at the front and rear, were pulled out to the grain field and loaded one by one with bundles to a height of roughly eight feet from the floor of the wagon. After being filled to capacity, they were driven to the thresher and parked beside it for the unloading process. The person unloading the wagon forked each bundle up to the thresher operator who then fed it into the mouth of the thresher. The threshing machine, which was noisy even when running idle, began a deafening roar that continued until all the bundles had been fed into its maw and the wagon was empty. Then another wagon was pulled next to the machine and the same process was repeated. The operation involved intense, hard labor in an extremely hot, noisy and dusty atmosphere.

The farm housewife, too, played an important role on threshing day. It was her responsibility to see that the twenty or more hardworking men were well fed at noontime. My mother often asked a couple of her sisters or neighbor ladies to help her prepare the large amounts of food necessary to feed the hungry throng. The usual menu for the thresher's lunch (I use the term advisedly because it had little resemblance to present-day lunches) included several kinds of meat, three or four cooked vegetables, several types of salads, mashed potatoes and gravy, three to five different kinds of pie, a cake or two, and gallons of coffee and lemonade. All of the foods were prepared from raw materials rather than having been purchased, ready-made, from a supermarket. The many different foods were cooked on a wood or coal burning kitchen range which also heated the kitchen to nearly unbearable temperatures during the already hot summer day.

The ladies set up several tubs of warm water on the back porch, with bar soap and towels nearby, where the dusty men washed before eating. In order that so many could eat at one sitting, every table in the household was called into use. Our dining room, even though rather large, was filled to capacity with the threshers. During the meal the women busied themselves with serving the food, replenishing the empty dishes and pouring coffee or lemonade. They and the children had their meal after the men had finished eating and had returned to the threshing operation.

Then loomed the gigantic task of cleaning up the aftermath! No paper goods were used at threshers' meals, so huge stacks of dirty dishes and silverware were washed and replaced in their cupboards. Pots and pans were scrubbed and put away, leftovers were taken care of and furniture was put back in its usual place. Floors were scrubbed, wash tubs were emptied and cleaned and a myriad of additional tasks were completed. Thankfully, the threshers ate their evening meal at home after finishing the day's work, so Mother and her helpers didn't have to begin preparing another meal immediately after cleaning up from the first one! Certain farms, however, produced enough grain acreage that the threshing process took more than one day, so the women of those households had to look forward to more of the same the following day. I don't recall any of our threshing operations extending beyond the first day.

No one in the farm family escaped his or her assigned duties on threshing day. Children, depending on their ages, had differing responsibilities. The girls usually helped with meal preparation and the cleanup that followed. Young boys supplied the workers in the field and those at the threshing machine with cool water to drink throughout the day. I know from personal experience that twenty or more thirsty men can drink a lot of jugs of water on a scorching summer day—water that had to be pumped by hand from the well and carried from the farm lot out to the field where the men were working. Older boys (perhaps twelve and above) worked in the field, alongside the men, tossing the grain bundles up on the wagons, arranging the grain on the wagon, or driving the tractors or teams of horses. My brother, Buddy, says his usual job was to shovel the grain in the nearly airless granary bins.

The threshing continued throughout the afternoon until the normal quitting time of 6:00 p.m. or until the last bundle of grain was processed. After having listened to the roar of the thresher all day, the ensuing silence was almost deafening and it took some time for one to adjust to the overwhelming quiet. My dad, as the farm owner, thanked each of his neighbors who had helped during the day and bade them goodbye as they pulled out of the driveway and made their way toward their respective farms. He settled up financially with the owner of the threshing machine, who also went on his way homeward. Thus another hectic threshing day came to a quiet end.

A few years after World War II ended in 1945, Dad bought a McCormick-Deering Company grain combine. That machine "combined" the two operations of cutting and threshing the grain into one single operation—thus the name. It made harvesting grain much simpler because it saved time and involved only a couple of workers. One person drove the tractor that both pulled the machine and provided its power source for threshing. The grain kernels collected in a *hopper*—a large container on the side of the combine. Another person operated a truck, with a grain box, into which the grain was poured when the hopper was filled. The straw was expelled out the rear of the combine onto the ground and later it was baled and hauled to the barn. By using that machine, two workers were able to accomplish what it had taken twenty previously! Additionally, there was no waiting time between cutting and threshing, therefore, the crop stood less chance of being ruined by inclement weather.

The combine was rather expensive and, because it was specialized (only able to harvest a few crops), Dad needed to find a way for the machine to fully earn its keep. He accomplished that by hiring himself and the combine out to neighboring farmers who were without one. As it happened I often was a part of the deal and went along to drive the truck for hauling the threshed grain. In that manner Dad was able to justify the expenditure of so much money for one machine. For several years we went from farm to farm combining grain during the harvest season. And, after I left the farm and began attending Michigan State, my younger brother, Dan, took my place at the wheel of the grain truck.

Such a contrast threshing day was for our customers from what it had been only a few years previously! The farmer was required to make few if any preparations prior to the day, itself. He merely had to have granary space available for storing the threshed grain if he were not going to put it on the market immediately. However, the farm owner often had me drive the loads of grain directly to town where it was purchased by the local grain elevator operator.

The wife of the farm owner, too, was relieved of much of her onerous responsibility on threshing day. She <u>did</u> provide meals for our threshing crew, but compared to feeding twenty or more as was previously necessary, having only two extra people at the table was rather insignificant. Thus a necessary and important rural institution, the threshing day (at least as I once knew it); disappeared forever from the farm scene.

CHAPTER 9

THE HOME COMFORT RANGE

Jerry R. Davis

THE HOME COMFORT RANGE

Growing up in rural Michigan during the Great Depression of the 1930's could be a lonely time for children and adults alike. People from the nearest town rarely if ever came out to the country to visit. In the spring of the year on the last day of school, I would bid my classmates goodbye and usually wouldn't see them again until the first day of school the following fall. In fact, because the times were very hard and money was in such short supply, few visitors ever darkened our doorstep. Most people were desperately trying to wrest at least a meager living from the soil or toil at some other equally difficult enterprise and there was little time for frivolous activities like visiting one's neighbors. That was especially true during the weekdays when everyone on a farm was either taking care of the animals in the barn and stable or working in the fields. If visitors should happen to appear they would find only the lady of the house present and likely she would be busy gardening or preparing meals. On Sundays there were occasional visit by aunts and uncles or other relatives who lived in larger cities within driving distance from our farm.

Probably the most frequent visitor to the farm during those years was a character who has nearly disappeared from the present scene— the traveling salesman. Throughout this narrative only the male gender will be used to designate the salesman because I never once heard of a traveling sales<u>woman</u> during my youth. Farm people who didn't have ready access to drugstores, supermarkets, hardware stores et cetera would depend on those nomadic businessmen to provide them with many of the necessities of life. They sold different types of non-perishable food items, medicines designed to cure, or at least ease, any number of ailments common at the time, cloth by the yard, sewing items like thread, needles and thimbles, and even larger goods such as furniture and appliances.

Before I was old enough to work in the fields with the men, my days were spent playing in and around the farm buildings. It was invariably a real cause for excitement when I saw a salesman turn into our driveway. Housewives, too, were willing, and possibly even eager, to set aside their work long enough to welcome the visitor, offer him coffee or a cool drink, and look over his assortment of goods for sale. Often he was delivering items which the housewife had ordered at the time of his previous visit, so that, too, added to the allure.

About once a month a Mr. Lewis, whom we called "The Raleigh Man," because he peddled products of the Raleigh Company, showed up at our farm in his sleek, black Model A Ford panel truck. As we clustered around him, he would spread his carrying case out on our kitchen table and display the many items he had for sale. One type of product that his company distributed was soft drink concentrates in various flavors to which we would merely add cold water and drink. There was no easy access on the farm to Pepsi Cola or Coca Cola products so the concentrates went a long way toward satisfying our soft drink needs.

The Raleigh Man always was a welcome visitor to our farm. We used the products that he sold in many ways and we enjoyed the companionship he provided on his monthly visits. For us children he had one added attraction. Often he would give us candy, which we really appreciated because we had it rarely.

Another salesman who visited us regularly was "The Watkins Man". The types of merchandise he peddled were very similar to those of the Raleigh Company. I still remember very well one particular item which he had in his collection. Among his patent medicines was a brand of cough syrup which was so vile tasting that it must have been effective in curing even the worst cough. To my way of thinking, it was pure rotgut! If my memory serves me correctly the concoction contained a fairly high concentration of alcohol and that was likely the taste to which I objected so strongly. However, not everyone shared my tastes, or lack thereof. A number of local people became rather fond of the syrup and used it regularly whether or not they suffered from a cough. Apparently taste, like beauty, is dependent on the participant.

"The Watkins Man" also sold Cod Liver Oil Pills. He touted them as being good for curing most of the ailments which might befall growing children. My mother believed every word of his spiel and bought a large supply of the ugly, brown things. She insisted that each of us take two before bedtime. For as long as I could remember I had an extremely difficult time taking any kind of pills. No matter how hard I tried I simply could not swallow them. After the introduction of the Cod Liver Oil Pills into our household, ingesting them became a nightly trauma for me as I vainly attempted to get them to go down my throat. Finally it got to the point that I would only pretend to swallow the hateful things, hold them in my mouth, trying not to upchuck, and then dispose of them later in secret. I recall looking under my bed and seeing a number of the pills lined up near the wall where I had dropped them. They looked like a row of caskets at a mass funeral! It is difficult for me to believe that my mother didn't see them when she cleaned, but if she did discover them, I never learned of it.

It was my assumption that the Watkins Company was a thing of the past as I had heard nothing about it for many years. Yet, my brother, who lives in the state of Washington, mentioned that he has seen its display booth recently at the Western Washington State Fair at Puyallup. I doubt that the company's present means of distribution includes any traveling salesmen of the genre described here, however.

The traveling salesman who made the most indelible impression on me visited our farm only once, *but he stayed an entire week!* One summer day as I was playing in the yard, a stranger appeared in our driveway. He was a jolly looking, roly-poly man with a big, brown cigar clamped in his teeth. His means of transportation was a single-seat buggy, with a black patent leather convertible top, pulled by a small, brown mare. My mother invited him into the house and we soon discovered his reason for being there. He was a sales representative for the Home Comfort Company and was peddling wood-burning kitchen ranges door-to-door. I have no idea how he knew ahead of time that he had come to the right place at precisely the right time, and perhaps he didn't, but that turned out to be the case anyway.

For months Mother had been complaining about the great, black, hulking monster of a stove that had occupied a prominent place on one side of our kitchen since well before I was born. My older brother, Buddy, remembers that range especially well because it was a *LAUREL* which was his correct first name. The stove's rusty cooking surface had a long crack that extended from front to back and it smoked badly. The temperature indicator on the oven door no longer worked so that my mother, who was a very good cook, managed to burn some of the pies and other foods she tried to bake in it. Even the poorest of salesmen could have sold Mother on a new kitchen range at that juncture. Our visitor was far from the poorest of salesmen as he had a gift of gab that put all of us in awe of him. And, in addition to his impressive sales pitch, he had a wondrous secret weapon in his arsenal of selling devices.

The secret weapon was a miniature sample range which was a source of continuing delight to my siblings and me. It was an exact replica of the full-sized stove that later arrived at our house. The model was about a foot square and was perfect in every detail even down to the tiny handles on the fire pit door and on the oven. We fell in love with it at first sight. I remember asking the salesman if we please could keep it as a toy when he was about to leave. He, of course, had to decline, much to our dismay. I have since seen a few of those sample stoves in antique shops around the country and they continue to fascinate me to this day. An interesting side note is that the miniatures now sell for many times what my parents paid for that full-sized range in the 1930's.

I don't know exactly why the salesman stayed for a week, but here is my hypothetical explanation for that turn of events. Perhaps he lived quite a distance away and used our home as a sort of headquarters for the next several days as he made his rounds offering his merchandise to all our neighbors. At that time there were few hotels and no motels in the vicinity from which he could have rented a room. He probably talked my parents into letting him park his horse and buggy in our barn and sleep in our guest room. As I said earlier, he had a good gift of gab and was a consummate salesman. I never did know what financial arrangements he made, but I do know that he was treated as an honored guest for his entire stay and even ate his meals with us. Meals, by the way, that were cooked on the old black kitchen range that was about to be replaced.

After the salesman left and went on to other prospective customers, we waited expectantly for the arrival of the new stove. At last, after about a month had elapsed, a big truck pulled into the yard with several boxes stacked in the back—none of which looked the right size to contain our new stove. The boxes did, in fact, turn out to hold the kitchen range all right, but before it would look like the one we had ordered, it had to be assembled. When it was finally put together and in place, that new stove became the pride of our kitchen.

Not only did the Home Comfort range provide a cooking surface for my mother to use, but it had a number of additional functions as well. Because the house had no furnace for central heating, the stove heated all of the rooms on that side of the house. The other side of the house was heated by a wood burning space heater in the living room. On cold mornings we would stampede down from our unheated upstairs bedrooms, open the oven door and toast our *derrieres* in front of it while we dressed ourselves. There were even times when we leaned too close and were painfully singed in the process.

A container called a reservoir was attached to the right side of the stove and it provided us with our only source of hot water in the entire house. One of my earliest assigned chores was to keep the reservoir filled at all times. The heat from the firebox warmed the water so that it was ready when needed. A usual Saturday night ritual involved ladling the heated water from that container into the wash tub in which we took our weekly baths. Looking back on the primitive conditions that existed in our rural area a scant sixty years ago, really makes me realize what great strides have been made during the past half century or so.

The range had two latched compartments situated near the central stovepipe and well above the cooking surface that were called warming ovens. My mother used to place heated foods there in order to keep them hot while she finished other meal preparations. They had another purpose—that of heating bread dough after it was placed in the bread pans. The heat made the bread rise. Thus the range not only cooked and baked the different foods but also provided additional services to the cook. The Home Comfort kitchen ranges certainly lived up to their names and did, indeed, provide comfort in the homes where they were found. Today's salesmen would be hard pressed to find a single product which could contribute so much in such a variety of ways.

I fear that both the wood burning kitchen range <u>and</u> the traveling salesman have gone the way of DeSoto automobiles and the big seventy-eight r.p.m. records. While I would not want to go back to life as it was when I was growing up on the farm, I can mourn its passing from the safety of my centrally heated and air conditioned home that has all the appliances that make Twenty-first Century living so very comfortable.

CHAPTER 10

THE IRON HORSES

THE IRON HORSES

Our family farm near Vassar had a very close relationship to the railroad. The tracks of the Michigan Central, a division of the New York Central Railroad, ran along the south side of our acreage. One of my first memories of that farm is lying in bed at night listening to the steam locomotives as they attempted to make their way up the rather steep grade just past our property. The farm was on the edge of Vassar, where the trains had stopped, so they had little distance to get up a good head of steam and speed enough to make the grade easily. I remember hearing them go slower and slower—"Chug, chug, chug, chug." Then, all of a sudden, the engine's power wheels would slip on the tracks—"Chuga, chuga, chuga, chuga!" Then, slowly, the engine would gain traction again and the slow—"Chug, chug, chug" would begin all over again. That was repeated over and over again until the train finally made it up the grade to the more level area beyond.

Our farm fronted on Vassar Road near where it crossed the railroad, and as I went to and from school, I walked the bridge daily. When a train was approaching, it was exciting to slip under the bridge and crouch on the slanted sides formed of cement that led down to the tracks below. If the train were approaching from the west, traveling downhill, it roared under the bridge and past me as I clung to the cement only a very few yards away. The engineer often saw me, and timed his whistle for the grade crossing coming up so that its scream resonated under the bridge and it seemed as if a wall of sound hit me full blast. That was scary but lots of fun. If the train were approaching from the east, and traveling uphill, it was interesting to see the drive wheels on the engine slip and send out a shower of sparks as they lost traction on the climb. Then the train would slowly inch along as it once again gained its footing.

That same railroad crossing bridge figured in an event in my life even before we moved to the Vassar farm. When we still lived near Tuscola, my parents would occasionally let me stay overnight in Vassar at my maternal grandparents' home. That was one of my favorite things to do because I really enjoyed spending time with my grandmother, who seemed unable to deny me anything that my heart desired. To me she was the best that the adult world had to offer. One morning after breakfast, Grandmother Williamson asked me if I would like to attend a bridge dedication. Being only seven years old, I had no idea what that was, but was willing to find out. Previously, Vassar Road crossed the railroad on a rickety wooden bridge, but the span had recently been replaced by a fine new cement structure. Grandmother and I went to the dedication and we enjoyed watching the parade, hearing the Vassar High School band play and listening to several speeches. Afterward, refreshments were served, too. Little did I know that a scant two years later, I would be living on the farm just on the north edge of the bridge, and that I would be crossing it daily as I walked to school.

A small spur of the main Michigan Central Railroad traveled from Vassar across much of Tuscola County, and it ran directly through our property. Its right of way effectively divided the farm into two parts. There were roughly 140 acres west and 100 acres east of the railroad.

When we pastured cows east of the tracks it was necessary, every day, to open the gates on either side of the right of way and drive them through. And the same was true for moving farm equipment from one side of the farm to the other. We always had to remember to keep both gates closed, otherwise, the pasturing horses and cattle could wander down the tracks and into Vassar, or up the tracks to a nearby road crossing.

Only one train traveled on the railroad spur that bisected the farm. Late each morning, after the cars were loaded with freight in Vassar, the train slowly made its way across our property. If any of us happened to be in the fields or pastures nearby, we always waved at the engineer and the men in the red caboose that followed behind. The little grade crossing on our farm had its own signal from the locomotive's whistle—one short blast. As the train left our property we could hear the signal blasts for the crossing at the next road beyond—two shorts and one long. The train traveled in a northeasterly direction toward Caro, the County Seat of Tuscola County, located sixteen miles away. After going through the switching process there, it headed back down the tracks in the opposite direction for its return trip. About four o'clock in the afternoon, the train once again crossed our farm just before it ended its run in Vassar. And, once again, we had the chance to wave at the trainmen as they made their way homeward, and to listen for the one short blast from the train's whistle as it approached our crossing.

There were some drawbacks to living on a farm that was crossed by a railroad, but there were even more positive aspects to it. Opening the gates whenever we had to take animals or equipment across was certainly a distinct drawback, but the tracks also were a source of fun. My siblings and I used to make a game of seeing how far we could walk on a single rail without falling off. We learned to carefully place one foot directly in front of another and to hold our arms away from our sides for balance. As we grew older, we learned that we could even go for a long way in one direction, then hop over to the opposite rail and make the return trip—all without falling off. We devised contests whereby we not only found out who could walk the rails the farthest, but also the <u>fastest</u>. We became adept enough that we could actually run down the track.

We also learned how to tell if the train were on its way toward us even though it was not yet in sight. When we pressed our ears to the track, we could sense a definite vibration if the train were within a mile or two of where we crouched. Much further away than that, we could sense nothing from the tracks. I never found out if we were actually hearing the movement of the train on the track or if we were merely <u>feeling</u> it.

The train gave us a big scare one Saturday afternoon. It was a nice summer day and my dad's younger sister, Norma, and her family were visiting from Flint. We had brought a picnic lunch to the swimming hole which was a dammed up wide spot in the creek that ran through the pasture near the railroad track. Norma's young son, Dalton, got away from the watchful eye of his mother and began walking on the tracks toward the north. He was able to go a long way before we became aware of his absence. We finally saw him far up the line. We put our ears to the track and, sure enough, a train was heading toward him! I remember our running as fast as we could and getting him off the track just as the train was rounding the bend onto our property. Dalton, though he was very young, likely would have had enough presence of mind to move off the tracks on his own, but we were very relieved anyway.

The Michigan Central Railroad was the route by which I left the state for the first time. In June of 1953 I set out for Germany to be an exchangee for nearly six months. I have an old photograph of me holding my suitcase and standing next to the train just prior to the trip. That picture appeared on the front page of the weekly *Vassar Pioneer Times* shortly after I left. After boarding the train in Vassar, and traveling a few hours across the Michigan countryside, I arrived in Detroit. Aunt Mamie, my mother's eldest sister, met me at the huge Detroit Railroad Station and helped me find the connecting train headed for Washington, D.C.

Exchangees from all over the United States met at the Capital for an orientation, and then traveled by train to Montreal, Canada where we boarded the Norwegian ship that was to take us to Bremerhaven, Germany. That exchangee experience provided me with a great many firsts. Not only was it my first time out of my home state, but it was my first ride on a train, my first time on an ocean-going vessel, and my first flight in an airplane. Also it was the first time I had been in a foreign country and the first that I had seen an ocean. The trip was a real "eye opener" for a twenty year old farm boy from Vassar, Michigan.

When I had finished my degree at MSU, I began teaching in different cities around the state, and gave little thought to the trains that had fascinated me so much as a child. Then, in 1990, I became curious to see the farm again. After an absence of about forty years, once again I walked through the back of what had been our cattle pasture. Almost everything had changed drastically. Part of the 100 acre field east of the tracks had become a parking lot for the fairgrounds. The former grazing area, west of the tracks, had grown up to woods, and the dam at the swimming hole had long since disappeared. Two things, however, remained exactly as I remembered them nearly a half century earlier—the railroad tracks and the little grade crossing. As I hiked along the right-of-way I attempted walking the rails again, and found that I could still do it, but not nearly as well as formerly. Apparently, in that aspect, I haven't improved with age. While I was there the train came by. It was a diesel instead of a steam locomotive, but, as before, the engineer waved, and he still gave the one short blast when approaching the old crossing.

Though the steam engines belched black smoke, made cacophonous noises, and their whistles shrieked, the trains on the tracks crossing our farm were always a pleasant and welcome sight. I have many good memories of those "Iron Horses" and the friendly men who worked on them.

CHAPTER 11

A WEEK AT
THE COUNTY FAIR

A WEEK AT THE COUNTY FAIR

When I was a child the most noteworthy of the summer highlights in our rural area of Michigan was the County Fair. It was held in the village of Caro which was the County Seat and was situated about sixteen miles northeast of Vassar. The fair took place during the third week of August when the Michigan summer is at its hottest and most humid. The weather, however, could not dampen our high spirits and excitement about having a week off from the chores and labor on the farm and taking part in one of our favorite activities.

My older brother and I usually exhibited our 4-H club Hereford steers at the fair and we stayed in a small tent right on the grounds. That way we were able to feed, water and groom the steers and do all the necessary things to prepare them for exhibition and judging. Many other boys stayed there too, and we had a regular "tent city" community for the entire week. An adult 4-H Club supervisor lived in one of the tents and served as our chaperone during the stay. He even conducted daily inspections in order to see that we were keeping everything clean and tidy. The supervisor awarded prizes for the best kept tent. Another of the chaperone's responsibilities was to see that we boys, who were teenagers, did not stay out too late at night, so he conducted a bed check at about midnight. Those who were absent for those checks were awarded demerits.

The Hereford steers that we exhibited at the fair did not actually belong to us 4-H members. We had earned the right to raise them at the previous year's fair in something called a "Calf Scramble." That event involved turning twenty-five teen-aged boys loose with twenty young steers in a large pen in front of the fair's grandstand. Each boy had a six-foot length of rope—he was to use it to capture a calf and tie it to the fence. Of course the calves were frightened by the twenty-five yelling boys running toward them and they stampeded all over the pen. The ensuing melee provided the grandstand audience with no end of amusement. A few boys were dragged across the ground desperately hanging on to ropes attached to young steers. Others wrestled the calves to the ground while they tried to put the ropes on them. Some boys were kicked and trampled in the chaos, but I never heard of anyone really being injured. A few bumps and bruises were the extent of the wounds. Finally, all twenty steers ended up tied to the fence next to twenty triumphant boys and the audience gave them a rousing cheer and round of applause.

The winning boys took the young steers home with them and during the next twelve months fed and cared for them, trained them to accept a halter and prepared them for being judged at the following year's fair. After they were judged and the grand champion chosen, the steers were auctioned to the highest bidder. From the money the boy received for his steer, he paid for the original cost of the calf (fifty dollars, if I remember correctly), and the balance he could keep as profit. The system worked out well for all concerned—except the unfortunate steer that was headed for slaughter.

Our mornings during the week of the fair were spent seeing to the needs of the livestock. We fed and watered the steers, removed the manure from their stalls, bedded them down with fresh, clean straw, gave them baths and combed the switches at the ends of their tails. The Herefords were housed in open-air barns so they were visible to the hundreds of fair visitors who traipsed through each day. We made certain that the animals always were clean and presentable for their public.

On judging day we took special pains to see that the steers were looking good. Not only did we bathe and comb them, but we put a type of oil on their hooves and horns to make them shiny. We curled and fluffed the long switches on their tails and made waves in the hair along their flanks. We were told that process made them appear heavier and more beefy to the judges. Likely the judges, who knew all about the animals, were not fooled very much by a few wavy hairs. We also shined their leather halters to which the lead ropes were attached. When the steers were as ready as we could make them, we watched them very carefully to see that they didn't mess themselves in any way while we waited for the call to bring them to the judging pavilion.

The cattle judges looked for a number of desirable physical characteristics in each of the show animals. Because the Hereford steers were beef animals, ideally they should have wide, stocky bodies, with fleshy backs and hindquarters. Their legs should be short and straight, and they should have thick necks and broad heads. Their fat should be evenly distributed throughout their square bodies and in their muscles. I have seen some judges place their hands on different parts of the animals' bodies in order to determine how firm their flesh was. As beef cattle ready for market and eventual slaughter, they should weigh somewhat over a thousand pounds.

Because the steers were being raised by us as projects, <u>we</u> also were judged in the show ring. During the previous year while we were raising the steers we were supposed to have spent a lot of time with the animals and trained them so that they were tractable and obedient. The judges even noted the animals' cleanliness, and if their hooves were cleaned and properly trimmed. Also, we were judged on how the steers responded to the lead rope and whether or not they remained still while being handled by the judge. The thrill of having one's steer win a beautiful purple grand champion ribbon made all the work and preparations worthwhile.

The afternoons during the fair week were usually considered free time for us. During those hours we often went to see the hundreds, perhaps thousands, of other exhibits the fair had to offer. Because I was interested in architecture and homes, I was especially fascinated with the house trailer and motor home displays. It always amazed me how many different appliances and pieces of furniture could be squeezed into an extremely small space—often no larger than one of our chicken coops. I thought it would be fun and challenging to design such conveyances. We spent hours in the merchant's building, the horse barns, the chicken and rabbit building, the pig barns and the vegetable and fruit hall. The vast variety of exhibits was almost overwhelming!

We seldom had the chance to see a carnival, so the sights along the fair's midway were a real treat for us. We attempted to win the plush toy animals by knocking over milk bottles or shooting air guns and many other games of skill. We rode on hair-raising rides that were designed to thrill or scare us—rides such as the Ferris wheel, the Tilt-a-whirl, the Dive bomber and the Roller coaster. We listened to the fascinating and vociferous spiels of the carnival barkers as they promoted their freak shows. The signs and drawings in front of those sideshows promised much, but after we paid our money and went inside, we soon learned that they delivered little that was truly notable.

Most of my fair experiences were very positive in nature, however, I recall one that turned out to be just the opposite. On that particular afternoon, I was standing before the booth where people were attempting to knock over milk bottles with a ball, and the booth owner asked me if I wanted a job. I didn't have anything important to do for a few hours so I accepted. Being rather young and naïve, I didn't discuss the pay I was to receive and, craftily, neither did he. The booth owner gave me a money apron and showed me how to set up the milk bottles correctly. The bottom bottles were heavily weighted but the top one was very light. Thus, one had to hit them in just the right place or one of the bottom bottles would remain standing. I was to sell the balls at four for a dollar, set the fallen bottles upright and give out prizes to the few customers who were successful in knocking over all three bottles. The owner, once he saw that I seemed to know what I was doing, took off for parts unknown and only returned to the booth a couple of times. I worked all afternoon and on into the evening—a total of about eleven hours. My conservative estimate would be that I took in $500 during that time. When the owner came back to the booth at closing time that night, he very generously gave me two quarters! All that stooping and bending was very tiring and for that I earned a little less than five cents per hour! The episode taught me a couple of things that have stood me in good stead throughout the ensuing years. First, don't accept a job until you know the particulars about it, and second, don't assume that everyone is as honest and aboveboard as you are. That was the beginning and also the end of my career as a Carnie!

After we had fed and watered the livestock and bedded them down for the night, we were free to take in some of the other events that the fair had to offer. At least once during the week we made it a point to attend the show at the grandstand. That usually consisted of musical presentations, clown antics, acrobats, high wire performers and trapeze artists. Occasionally, movie stars like Gene Autry or Roy Rogers put on a show for the audience. I was always amazed when anyone famous appeared at our little county fair, but it did happen.

The county 4-H Clubs owned and operated a food stand at the fair each year. It was run by the club members under the guidance and direction of a 4-H adult leader. Usually an older club member, perhaps eighteen to twenty years old, was selected as the student manager of the operation. His or her job was to see that there was volunteer help available for each of the shifts, arrange for food deliveries, bank the proceeds at the end of each day and, in general, keep the business in good order. I spent much of my free time working at the stand. I waited on customers, washed dishes, cleaned counters, took cash and scrubbed pots and pans. But, I never cooked. That is an undertaking that I still don't involve myself in to this day. Thankfully, the manager never asked me to help out in that area, as I would probably have been forced to refuse.

I feel that running the business was a positive and constructive enterprise for the 4-H Club members in a number of ways. The profits from the business paid for some of our yearly outings, it provided us with some practical experience in running a business, and it gave us a chance to meet the public and deal face to face with, not only customers but, suppliers too. We learned business lessons in the venture that would serve us well in the future. And, as an added bonus, it was fun!

When the week of the fair was over, I was exhausted. The heightened excitement and activities of those few days really took their toll on my energies. However, I wouldn't have traded the experience for anything on earth. The week's stay at the fair provided many memories to entertain and carry me through the following year, and I could look forward to the next one with eager anticipation.

A few years ago I drove to Caro and attended the fair for the first time in at least thirty years. Though everything seemed smaller to me, I still felt the thrill and excitement of the varied activities. I watched the cattle judging and saw both the triumph of the winning entrant and the agony of defeat of the losers. Later I ate a hamburger and piece of pie at the 4-H food stand. I was amused at the very earnest, but inefficient boy who waited on me. He could have been me nearly fifty years previously! I listened to the absurd claims of the carnival barkers along the midway and they hadn't changed a bit. When I saw a young lad working in the booth with the milk bottles, I hoped that he had more astute business sense than I had when that job was mine. For me it was a very pleasant and nostalgic trip down memory lane.

CHAPTER 12

A TWO-ROOM
EDUCATION

Jerry R. Davis

A TWO-ROOM EDUCATION

My first home was a farmhouse about a mile north of the village of Tuscola which lies astraddle the slow-moving Cass River that meanders its way in a southwesterly direction through Tuscola County, Michigan. In the 1930's Tuscola had a total population of about two hundred people and boasted two general stores, a gas station, a pool hall and beer garden, a library, an I.O.O.F. Hall, a church, a creamery and a school. Today the number of business places has shrunk, but the population has burgeoned to about three hundred inhabitants. When I was a child the main street through the village was paved with asphalt, but the rest of the streets were gravel covered.

Near Tuscola's center was an irregularly shaped plot of land on which the school sat. Much has been written about the ubiquitous one room schools in rural America, but ours was a cut above those because it had two classrooms. The school was erected during the middle of the 1800's in the then popular Greek Revival Style. It was sided with white clapboards and across the entire front was a long, columned porch which had cement steps at either end. I nearly ruined my first bicycle riding it down those steps—bump, bump, bump. That activity was exciting but jarring.

The school's interior was made up of the "Little Room" where pupils from the kindergarten through the fifth grade attended classes, the "Big Room" where grades six through eight were taught, a girls' cloakroom, a boys' cloakroom and a communal chemical toilet. In a

112

corner of each classroom stood a huge (to me anyway), round coal-burning furnace that required stoking several times daily. Fred Honnel, who lived across the street, was hired as the official janitor and it was his responsibility to keep the fires burning, the classrooms cleaned and the porch cleared of snow. One time Fred was teasing one of my classmates, Shirley Sohn, by pulling on her fingers. Shirley couldn't as yet pronounce all her consonants correctly and she screamed, "Oh, Tred, my tore tinger!"

School began for me a little less than a month after my fifth birthday. My brother, Buddy, had been attending for two years by that time and I was envious that he was able to go and I wasn't. At that tender age time passed very slowly—a year was an aeon and two years seemed an eternity. At last the long awaited day arrived and I was able to walk with Buddy as he made his way to school. He appeared totally unimpressed, but I was antsy with anticipation.

There were five rows of school desks in our classroom that spanned the room from front to back. The kindergarteners and first graders sat in the row nearest the windows, the second graders were in the next row and so on across the room. The recitation bench and teacher's desk occupied the west side of the room in front of the chalkboard. The recitation bench was a long wooden seat with a back that could hold an entire grade of pupils at one time. The grades usually were from three to five pupils in number depending on the year.

Each time the teacher was ready for a certain grade to do its recitation work in the front of the class she would say, for example,

"Third graders rise." They would stand. Her next command was, "Third graders pass." They would file to the front of the classroom and stand in front of the recitation bench with their backs to it. Then she would say, "Third graders sit." And they would comply. During their recitation period they would be expected to show that they had studied the assigned lessons for the day, after which the entire standing and passing procedure would be repeated only in reverse.

While one grade was reciting, the rest of the students were expected to attend to their own lessons at their seats. Of course they could hear every word that was exchanged in the front of the room, so they often would learn information about lessons which perhaps they wouldn't be studying until the following year or so. Conversely, if they had missed some information in years past it would be possible for them to have remedial instruction merely by listening. That made for an extremely efficient educational system.

Toilet privileges were granted but very sparingly. Rather than a pupil merely getting out of his seat and going to the toilet when he had to answer a call of nature, it was required instead that he go through a specified procedure. First he must raise his hand and the number of fingers he held up would depend on which call of nature he was intending to answer. When he had a pressing need to urinate he would hold up only one finger, but if Mother Nature were telling him that he had to do more than "tinkle" then he held up two fingers! Sixty years later I still use those designations by saying that I have to go "number one" or "number two." If the pupil had not asked to go to the toilet too often in the past, then permission was usually granted.

Never have I been able to ascertain why it was necessary for the teacher to know if the pupil were going to urinate or defecate, moreover, how would she use the information once she knew it? For me those weighty questions make up one of life's little conundrums.

Kindergarteners in our school attended classes all day instead of only a half day as is the present practice. They were kindergarteners for only one semester and became first graders at the end of that time. The first grade, too, lasted only one semester and when the pupils began their second year of school they advanced into the second grade. I started school shortly after reaching five years of age and, because of that half year system, was graduated from high school when I was only sixteen. I found that to be a rather mixed blessing. I was one to two years younger than my classmates and probably too young and immature when I began college at such a young age.

My first teacher was a lady named, Bessie Davis. She too was a descendant of my great great grandparents so we were distant cousins. The fact that our last names were the same made not the slightest difference to Miss Davis. She expected me to do my schoolwork with a minimum of nonsense the same as any other pupil under her tutelage. I was an eager student and anxious to learn so we fared well together. In 1938, when I was in the third grade, Miss Davis became seriously ill and bedridden with pneumonia a short time before the school Christmas vacation was to begin. Because of Miss Davis's illness, we were dismissed early that year.

Soon Miss Davis was sent to a nearby city hospital where she lapsed into a coma from which she never recovered. She died late in

Jerry R. Davis

December when I was only seven years old and was the first of my personal acquaintances to do so. That was a shock for me and it left a deep impression on my young mind. Here is an interesting side note: Miss Davis had seemed old from the first time I saw her, but when I visited her grave in the Davis plot of the Tuscola Cemetery recently, I was quite surprised to learn that she was only fifty-two at the time of her death. How the mere passage of years can alter one's frame of reference!

In spite of Miss Davis's death, the pupils still were required to attend school, so a new teacher was hired. Before meeting the replacement we students were consumed with curiosity about her and in no way were we disappointed. Miss Claudia Piazza was her name and she was a nineteen year old girl from nearby Vassar. The sum total of her teacher training consisted of attending one year of Tuscola County Normal School. She was very attractive and even more impressive, she was young! Her youth and lack of teacher training, however, didn't detract from her ability to do the job for which she had been hired. She was serious about teaching and, though she made us work hard, we thoroughly enjoyed her classes.

After I became a teacher I taught for a number of years in a junior high school in Saginaw—a city in the adjoining county to the west from Tuscola. I occasionally ran across Miss Piazza (who was Mrs. Barnes by that time) at teacher conferences. In the intervening time she had earned her academic degrees through years of part-time course work at various universities. The two of us enjoyed reminiscing about the good old days when I was her pupil and she was my teacher.

About five years ago, after I had been retired from teaching for ten years, I visited Mrs. Barnes and her husband in Vassar. She was well into her seventies, but was still the same attractive and vivacious person who had impressed me so when I was a child. Hopefully I have aged as gracefully as she.

In 1942, when I was nine years old, my dad sold the farm near Tuscola and bought another just north of Vassar and our family moved from the place I had lived all my young life. That necessitated changing schools too. The Vassar school was much larger than the two room school to which I was accustomed. For example, each grade had an <u>entire</u> room to itself rather than sharing space with four others. The numbers of students and size of the building caused me to suffer some culture shock at first, however I adjusted quickly and soon felt at home in the new school.

Recently I drove through the village of Tuscola and looked at the many changes that have taken place there. At present there is only one general store in town, no gas station, no creamery, no beer garden and pool hall and no library. The I.O.O.F. Hall still stands and now there are two churches instead of only one. A new post office was built along with a sporting goods store, and a small cabinet shop. All of the streets in town have been paved with asphalt. A new four room brick school was built in the 1960's, but now that too is abandoned because all Tuscola pupils are bussed the five miles or so to the Vassar Public Schools. The schoolyard in the center of the village was subdivided into several lots and there is a house on each of them. The old two room school that I attended was renovated into a two-story apartment house with four apartments.

Though the two room school, as such, no longer exists, an active remnant of it still survives. Each year in September, the old I.O.O.F. Hall echoes with the festive sounds of the former students of the Tuscola School meeting together for our annual reunion. Each year our ranks diminish and like the school, someday we all will be gone.

CHAPTER 13
ANATOMY OF AN INFERIORITY COMPLEX

THE ANATOMY OF AN INFERIORITY COMPLEX

The events that make up the following story are very painful for me even to think about and I find writing about them next to impossible. The episode resulted in a dramatic change in my outlook, my psyche and the very core of my being. Little wonder that it is difficult to find the words to put it down on paper. But, I may as well just go ahead and start and see how it comes out.

When I was a young child, I was outgoing and gregarious. I was interested in the world around me and enjoyed the company of others—children and adults alike. I had positive feelings of self-confidence and self worth. The world, including its inhabitants, was my oyster and I relished it. On a particular day when I was ten years old and in the sixth grade at Vassar Public Schools, much of that was to change.

My teacher that year was Miss Florence Reed, a spinster who lived with her bachelor brother on the east side of town. She had been teaching for many years—in fact she had taught my mother and my mother's older sisters in the same room twenty-five to thirty years previously. She was a very strict and uncompromising teacher who kept her pupils under rigid control. She brooked no nonsense in the classroom and, because she had established a reputation years ago, few students ever challenged her.

On that particular day when I was working on some schoolwork at my desk, Miss Reed called my name and ordered me to come to her desk at the front of the classroom. I, of course, complied immediately.

When I approached her she asked if I helped my father with the milking of our cows in the mornings before coming to school. As it happened I had just begun doing that a short time previously and felt rather proud of the fact, and I answered in the affirmative. Miss Reed's next comment stunned me! She said, "I thought so. We've had complaints that you smell like a cow barn!" I was certain that all of my classmates heard the remark and I was mortified. In that instant the friendly world I had known collapsed. Somehow I managed to find my way back to my seat where I sat down and hung my head in abject shame. While sitting there I thought to myself that nothing could have been more embarrassing to me than her making such a statement. But I was wrong because things did get worse!

In a short time we students were dismissed by Miss Reed for the fifteen minute afternoon recess and all of us filed out into the schoolyard. It was then that my misery was compounded. All that remains with me from those fifteen minutes is the terrible memory of some of the other pupils circling me and shouting, "Jerry smells like a cow barn!" "Jerry smells like a cow barn!" over and over and over again. That is one of the very few times in my life that I have ever felt that death would be preferable to living.

That evening at home I told my parents what happened. They were very sympathetic but felt that little could be done after the fact. My dad went to the school the next day and confronted Miss Reed, but that did no good—the damage already done was irreparable at that point in time. Had she been inclined to make a public apology, which she wasn't, it would have only drawn more attention to my humiliation and made me feel worse. Miss Reed, of course, felt that she had done nothing out of the way or wrong, so she displayed no contrition. As far as she was concerned we should simply take care of the cow barn smell and go on as before. She had no hint of what damage she had done to me and my self esteem.

Thirteen years later, when I began my own teaching career in the same school in the classroom directly beneath the one where the incident occurred, I vowed that I would <u>never</u> commit such a callous and indifferent act toward any of my students. After teaching for thirty-one years, I can state with confidence that I lived up to my vow. Teachers may influence their students, both positively and negatively, in a wide variety of ways. They should take that responsibility seriously and make certain their actions cause no harm to the fragile psyches placed in their care.

I date the beginning of my inferiority complex to that hideous incident. From then on I became introverted and no longer enjoyed meeting and being with people as much as I had previously. I felt that I simply wasn't as worthy or as good as others. Furthermore, I was certain that everyone felt the exact same thing about me. My school life continued in the company of those same students until we were graduated six years later, but I never made any close friends among my classmates. I was convinced that I was an outcast.

I always had been an avid reader, but after that I immersed myself in books. They became my safe haven—my world. Books spurred my very active imagination and transported me to wondrous places far removed from the surroundings in which I found myself. Books were never judgmental, but always supportive. They didn't look down on me, instead they accepted me exactly as I was.

During my high school years I became very active in the county 4-H Clubs. That is an organization which was developed for farm boys and girls from ages ten to twenty. We were involved in a number of individual and group projects connected with farming. My projects included such activities as raising pigs, raising cattle, home improvement, farm electricity, tractor maintenance and many others. We exhibited our animals and other projects yearly at the County Fair in the neighboring town of Caro. Group camps were held at Higgins Lake, and social events like square dances and roller skating parties were organized for us. We went to workshops in various locations around Michigan, and learned parliamentary procedures by holding offices in various chapters of the organization.

Because few of my school acquaintances lived on farms, my 4-H Club companions were not my classmates. Most of the club members attended schools in the more rural towns and villages around the county. Therefore, I felt no stigma in my associations with them. They were not aware that as a sixth grader I "smelled like a cow barn." I felt at ease and could make friends with them. Slowly my feelings of inferiority and insecurity began to disappear—at least when I was with my 4-H Club friends.

After high school I attended Michigan State University and when I was a junior was selected to represent Michigan 4-H Clubs and the United States State Department as an exchangee to Germany. Altogether I spent six months in Europe—most of it in Germany, but in addition I managed to visit England, France, Monaco, Austria and Italy. During the year following my return from Europe, I gave speeches to a number of different farm organizations around Michigan, describing my experiences abroad. By that time my inferiority complex was, for the most part, a thing of the past.

I find it interesting that those feelings still do rear their ugly heads once every five years. That occurs when my high school graduating class has its reunions. At those get-togethers, when I see certain classmates (those who were in that sixth grade classroom on that infamous day), some of my old insecurities re-emerge.

CHAPTER 14

SEVEN ROOMS
AND PATH

Jerry R. Davis

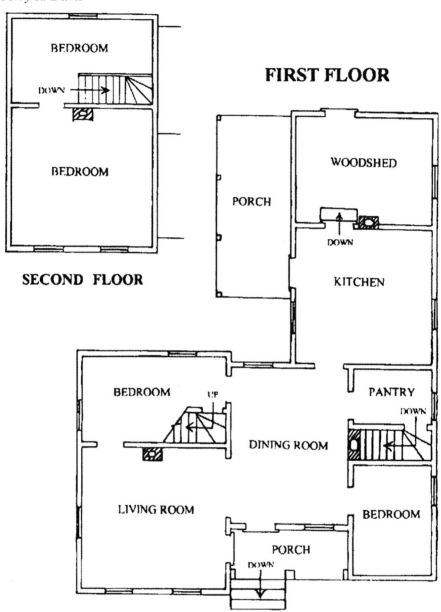

SECOND FLOOR

FIRST FLOOR

SEVEN ROOMS AND PATH

Farmhouses in the rural area of Michigan where I grew up during the 1930's and 1940's were a far cry from what they are today. Often they were large, so space for a six-member family was plentiful, but what was lacking were the comforts that we now expect our homes to include. The houses that I lived in were utilitarian rather than ornamental. They provided basic shelter and little else.

My family lived in two different farmhouses during my childhood. The house in which I was born was located about a mile north of the village of Tuscola on Van Cleve Road. The house was constructed during the mid 1800's and it was added on to during the latter part of that century. The Greek Revival style of architecture was all the rage in Michigan from 1840 to 1860, so the builder followed the then current trend. It had a tee-shaped plan with a one story wing attached at right angles to a two story wing. The added wing joined the one story section at the rear. On the front of the one story part there was a columned porch that had doors leading into the living room on the left and the dining room straight ahead. At the back of the house another porch led to the kitchen situated in the newer wing. Under the porch was a barrel-shaped, brick cistern for collecting rain water that could be dipped from a round trap-door in the porch floor.

Originally the house was painted white, but by the time we lived there, most of that paint had weathered off the clapboards and they had gained the gray patina common to barn wood. The windows were what is called "six over six" which means that there were six panes of glass in both the top and bottom sashes. At one time all the windows had green moveable shutters at their sides, but after nearly a hundred years of little or no upkeep, only a few of them remained. The remaining vestiges of landscaping included a large lilac tree at the front of the two story section, a bramble of rose bushes next to the driveway and a few large hardwood trees in the front yard. The lawn was grassy, but was only cut once or twice each summer when Dad used the field mower on it.

The house encompassed about fifteen hundred square feet on two floors. The first floor comprised a dining room, a living room, two bedrooms, a pantry, a kitchen, a woodshed and two stairways—one to the second floor and the other to the partial basement. The small second floor had two rooms—one was a large bedroom on the front over the living room and the other was the stairway hall that we used as a bedroom, too.

The most used front door led into the large dining room. That room served almost as a hallway because it was in the center of the house and had doors leading to nearly all the rooms on the first floor. In total, there were <u>nine</u> openings of some type from the dining room-cum-hallway. One window looked out on the front porch and another on the back porch. One door led to the porch and others to the living room, my parents' bedroom, the kitchen, the pantry and a small bedroom on the south. In the center of the south side of the room was a chimney which came down about four feet from the ceiling under which stood a built-in, storage cabinet with glass doors. Still there was enough space for a large dining room suite with a table and eight chairs, a buffet and a china cupboard, plus my mother's sewing machine.

In contrast the living room, which also had a door off the front porch, was rather sparsely furnished with a davenport and two matching chairs and a small table or two. Against the back wall of the room was a wood-burning space heater that provided warmth for that side of the house. The living room boasted an area rug on the floor that was surrounded with linoleum painted to look like hardwood flooring. However it failed to convince me or anyone else that it was anything other than inexpensive linoleum!

My parents' bedroom, directly back of the living room, was a very small ell-shaped room that wrapped around the winding stairway to the floor above. There was barely room enough for a double bed, a dresser, a small cardboard closet and a baby's crib. All three of my siblings and I were born in that room. One of my earliest memories is hearing my younger brother, Dan, crying shortly after he was born. I was just under four years old at the time.

The big kitchen, situated directly behind the dining room, was the real heart and soul of the house. Most of our visitors by-passed both of the front doors and came around to the back and were admitted through the kitchen door. The kitchen had a wood-burning range that dominated the east wall and provided the only heat source for that part of the house. A large oval table stood in the center of the room around which we ate most of our meals. It was at that table, too, where we did school homework, read magazines and books, drew pictures, discussed whatever topics interested us and helped Mother by shelling peas, husking sweet corn, cleaning strawberries, et cetera.

When my mother and dad bought the Tuscola farm and moved into the house, Mother was pregnant with my older brother, Buddy. The house had no electricity, running water, central heating, insulation or inside bathroom. All reading at night was done next to a kerosene or oil lamp. All water used in the house was pumped by hand at a well beneath a windmill in the back yard or dipped from the cistern. We took our weekly baths in a washtub near the kitchen range. The laundry was washed in a gasoline-powered Maytag washer and it was dried on clotheslines strung behind the house. Ironing was done by heating several irons on top of the kitchen range and then using them until they became too cool to be effective. Because we lacked a refrigerator, food that needed cooling was kept in a water tank in the milk house across the driveway from the house. To use the toilet we went out the back door and down a path to the privy. During the bitterly cold Michigan winters, the winds blew nearly uninhibited through cracks in the walls of the house. The bedrooms had little or no heat which necessitated our piling on many layers of quilts and blankets. I feel certain that a woman expecting her first child in the present day would find such living conditions utterly impossible, but Mother seemed to accept her lot with equanimity. And, we children were born into those conditions and knew nothing else so we, too, were content.

During the twelve years my family lived in the farmhouse we improved it in only a few ways. Probably the most important of the renovations was wiring the house for electricity. I remember watching the electricians for several days as they worked in and around the house drilling holes, fishing metal-clad wires through the walls and ceilings, and attaching the wires to light fixtures, switches and outlets. I was about four or five years old at the time and found the whole process very interesting. Fourteen years later, after I had finished my first year at Michigan State, I took a year off from college to work and earn money in order to go back for another year. During most of the hiatus I was employed by Bob Temple, who owned Vassar Electric Company, and I helped with many wiring jobs similar to the one undertaken at our old farmhouse.

What a difference electricity made! We were then able to make our lives easier and more comfortable by getting a refrigerator, an electric iron, a radio, electric lamps and many other appliances. An electric motor replaced the gasoline motor in the washer. We still didn't have central heating, insulation, hot and cold running water or an inside bathroom, but we felt that we had made great strides in spite of those inadequacies. To use the current common parlance, we were upwardly mobile!

The only improvement we made to the farmhouse, other than adding electricity, was replacing the door between the living room and dining room with a rounded arch. At that early age I was already interested in architecture and building so I really enjoyed watching the carpenter cut the larger opening through the wall, and form the 2 X 4 framework for the arch and then nail lath over the surfaces. When the carpenter was finished the plasterer took over the project. He mixed up a batch of plaster in a wooden trough. Then he troweled on an undercoat of the gray, soupy material. After that coat had dried a day or so; he came back and carefully applied the smoother, final coat. I still marvel at the ability that plasterers have to blend newly applied plaster to that which has been there a while and make it look as though the entire job was done in one operation. They are real artists!

In 1942, after my family had lived in the Tuscola farmhouse for twelve years, my dad sold the farm and we moved to another on the north edge of Vassar. For the next fifty years or so I often drove by the old farmhouse but never had any occasion to go inside. Then in the early 1990's my curiosity got the better of me and I drove in the yard and rapped on the screened door of the kitchen. A weak male voice called out for me to come in. I did so and found a man, who was an invalid, in the dining room lying on a recliner chair. I introduced myself and told him that I had been born in the house and spent the first nine years of my childhood living there. I told him about my curiosity to see the place after a lapse of fifty years. He was very gracious and told me to look around all I wanted. I was afraid of disturbing him, but did want to see the old house so I took a very short tour. The rooms were much the same as they had been when we moved out, except that hot and cold running water had been added and the pantry off the dining room had been remodeled into a bathroom. It was obvious that the house had suffered from decades of neglect, so it was not a pretty sight, but it did serve to stir up a lot of memories, both happy and sad, of my childhood.

Within a year from the time I visited the farmhouse, the invalid, who was renting it, died and the house was put up for sale. It sold almost immediately, I later learned, probably because the asking price was only $6,000. That price included the house and about an acre or so of property surrounding it. A middle-aged couple from a small town near Flint, Michigan bought the house and immediately began to make changes. They re-roofed it, put in a new electrical service, stripped off all the plaster and lath from the inside and cleaned up the yard. I stopped in one day while they were working on the place and learned that they intended to remodel the house and make it their home. The gutted farmhouse looked totally different from what it did the other times I had been there.

From then on when I drove past the farmhouse, all the activity in and around the place seemed to have ceased. The gutted shell remained in exactly the same condition that it had been when I last talked to the new owners. For some reason, unknown to me, they had abandoned the project. When I visited Michigan about a year ago the old farmhouse was still in a state of limbo. It made me melancholy, as I had been enthused about the prospect of the house where I was born being revamped and continuing to provide shelter for a Twenty-first Century family.

CHAPTER 15

DOWN TO THE PRIVY

DOWN TO THE PRIVY

Many Michigan farmhouses during the 1930's and 1940's had indoor toilet facilities, but neither of the two farmhouses in which I grew up was so blessed. When we had to go to the toilet it meant that either we used the "thunder mug" which resided under the bed or we went outside and down the path behind the house to the privy. My mother and sister used the "mug" at night but we males felt that it was more "macho" to go outside. Upon occasion people have said to me they wish they had grown up on a farm. When they say that, I wonder to myself just how much they would have enjoyed using outdoor facilities both summer <u>and</u> winter as we did. For me it didn't take very many trips to the privy before all the allure and romance of rural living had disappeared forever.

It is a fact of life that one must use the toilet during the cold as well as the warm seasons of the year. Michigan winters are known for being severe—daytime temperatures often go no higher than the twenties, and nighttime temperatures can drop well below zero. Those frigid winters came along each year and made our visits to that little building unpleasant. As far as I'm concerned, there is no way that sitting on a cold wooden bench, "mooning" the accumulation below while attempting to relieve oneself, can be either a gratifying or stimulating experience. I remember holding back answering the call of nature just as long as I could, then rushing out the back door down to the frigid building and taking care of my business as quickly as possible before running back up the path to the house to warm up near the big old kitchen range.

Sometimes I rebelled from having to go outside to relieve myself during the winters, but I still adamantly refused to use the thunder mug. I recall waking up in the unheated upstairs bedroom under a pile of quilts that was keeping me toasty, and realizing that I had to tinkle! The prospect of getting out from under the warm covers, dressing in the freezing room, going downstairs, finding a flashlight and going outdoors in the sub-zero temperature to the outhouse was daunting. Instead I got out of bed, opened the window on the back of the house and watered the snow from that lofty site. What blessed relief! And, even better, I was back in my cozy bed within seconds after finishing. My parents, to my knowledge, never found out about those incidents—which is just as well because I'm certain that they would not have appreciated my efficiency as much as I did.

Summer visits to the outdoor john were not as uncomfortable as those in the winter, but they were far from pleasant. Warm weather encouraged the putrefaction of the fecal matter and the resulting stench was nearly overpowering. The only creatures that enjoyed the odor were the swarms of flies that feasted there daily. They were extremely friendly to us and often landed on our exposed nether regions for an after dinner dessert consisting of a tidbit of human derriere. Our privy was near a slow-moving creek where mosquitoes hatched by the thousands and they, too, enjoyed our presence, though it was not reciprocated.

Visiting the privy in the summer time was an unpleasant trial, but even worse, was cleaning out the reeking mess that collected under it. Thankfully, I was never assigned that odious task. However, my dad, who obviously is made of sterner stuff, faithfully once a year parked the horse-driven manure spreader behind the structure, then shoveled the smelly accumulation into the vehicle and spread it on the fields. I tried to stay as far away as possible during the entire process.

We used the Sears and Roebuck Catalog in the place of toilet tissue but it was a poor substitute at best. The yellow pages of the index worked much better than did the pages with the pictures, because they were softer and more porous, however they were a far cry from Cottonelle Tissue. I always used up the index first before going on to the dreaded picture pages. Those pages served the purpose somewhat better when they were wadded up and then smoothed out before use. During the winter, with temperatures below zero, placing those smooth, cold papers against one's bottom could be a shocking experience. Worst of all were the pages with colored pictures on them. They were not only cold to the touch, but often left part of their colors behind after use. Sometimes we went around with technicolor tushes after visiting the privy.

Privies came in a wide variety of sizes, shapes and colors. The one on our first farm near the village of Tuscola was rather mundane. The little building was about four feet from front to back and about five feet from side to side. It was what is referred to as a "three holer." In other words three people, if they were so inclined, could use it at once. I have no idea just why they would be so inclined, but that is beside the point. It was built of vertical boards with battens covering the cracks between the boards. The cold winter winds still found their way through, however. The exterior was unpainted so its siding had weathered to a soft gray patina. Of course there was no electricity in the structure—the only light was provided by a small window situated high up on one wall. One's privacy was not assured as there was no lock on the inside of the door. As privies go, it was far from spectacular.

I drove by the Tuscola farm last summer when I was visiting Michigan. The house still remains even though it has been gutted in preparation for remodeling. In a tangle of of overgrown brush down a slight slope behind the house the old privy is just visible. The portion of the small building that I could see looked just the same as it did when it was such a necessary part of our lives many years ago. What it lacked in size, shape and style it made up for in longevity.

The outhouse on our second farm, the one near Vassar, was far different. That farm had been homesteaded in 1861 by Justin Wentworth, one of the early settlers of Vassar. He had been very successful in business and spared no expense in providing his family with the comforts of life when he built his farm buildings. One of those comforts was a fine privy. It was about seven feet from front to back and about eight feet from side to side. That privy was a "five holer"—there were three adult size holes at the rear and two child size holes on the left side near the door. Just as I can't imagine three people using the facility concurrently, even less can I imagine _five_ individuals sitting there at the same time. The outhouse was built in the Greek Revival Style, the same as the main house. It was sided with pale cream colored clapboards and was trimmed in forest green. The color scheme, too, was a perfect echo of that on the house.

The privy's interior walls were covered with horizontal tongue and grooved paneling, and for light, it boasted a frosted window located on the south side. Someone in the past had even attempted a little interior decoration because a number of pictures of Victorian ladies were glued to the walls at about eye level around the inside. At one time each of the five holes had a wooden lid that could be lowered when it was not in use, but by the time we bought the farm the lids were gone and only a few of their hinges remained.

I have an old book entitled, *History of Tuscola and Bay Counties, Michigan: Illustrated,* published in 1883, and on page twenty-two is a drawing of the Justin Wentworth residence and farm buildings. The house, barns, and other outbuildings are all easily recognizable in the drawing, and the artist did not fail to include the all important privy!

I'm gratified that the house and outbuildings have been at least somewhat preserved in the history book because most of them, including the outhouse, were torn down shortly after my dad sold the place in the 1960's and retired from farming. A modern house now stands where the old one did and a grassy lawn covers the spot where the privy once stood.

The outdoor toilet occasionally figured into local Halloween pranks too. I've heard stories of them being tipped over *with occupants still inside!* It takes little imagination to picture the resulting mess. One year, on the morning after Halloween when we arrived at the Vassar school, we were greeted by a privy sitting on the sidewalk right at the front door! Also a buggy was on top of the school, and live chickens were roaming around inside the building creating their own special kind of chaos. Though it is fun to make jokes about the old outhouses, I'm certainly happy that they have been replaced by modern, indoor bathrooms and that it is no longer necessary to use them in our daily living.

CHAPTER 16

WINTER WONDERLAND

Jerry R. Davis

WINTER WONDERLAND

Michigan is well known for having cold and dreary winters. The average January temperature in the mid-Lower Peninsula area where I lived is 23 degrees. However, I remember several times when the temperature dropped to 30 degrees <u>below</u> zero. The normal snowfall of that region in winter is slightly less than four feet. When one travels north into the Upper Peninsula, conditions worsen. The average January temperatures are lower and the usual snowfall is about thirteen and a half feet in a season. Annual snowfalls of up to <u>fifty</u> feet have been recorded. The Great Lakes nearly surround the state, and they affect the climate and weather of the area significantly. The skies over Michigan are at least partly cloudy on an average of seven out of every ten days in winter. The first time I traveled back to Michigan after moving to the Southwest, I spent ten days there during the Christmas and New Year's Day holiday season. The sun did not break through the heavy cloud layer until the tenth day of my visit—the day I was to leave.

The cold and snowy winters had a definite effect on my family when I was a child. Our house had no central heating and was totally without insulation. It was extremely hard to heat because the two wood or coal burning stoves—the only heat sources—simply were not up to the task. The house faced the west, the direction from which the prevailing winds blew, and I remember feeling the cold drafts that came through its many cracks. The upstairs bedrooms, where my brothers and I slept, had no heat source whatsoever. If we perchance left a glass of water on the bedside table at night, it would be ice covered by morning. I remember admiring the beautiful and varied patterns made by the frost on the windows. There were swirls and flourishes, straight lines, snowflake shapes and contrasting areas of transparence and translucence. The artistry lasted until the sun melted it in the morning. The windows truly were "frosted glass."

The Vassar farm was situated about a mile north of the school and we walked the distance between the two. A mile can seem as though it is extremely long to a ten year old boy as he is plodding his way through the unplowed snow on the side of the road, while attempting to protect his face from the cold winds cutting across his path. I sometimes envied those children who lived far enough away from the school that it was necessary for them to ride the bus each day. The school bus often passed me as I waded through the wintry accumulation.

One of our farm neighbors, Howard Gaunt, who lived on the second farm north of ours, sometimes gave me a ride if he happened to be going that way at the right hour. One time in particular, he both amused and frustrated me as he showed his concern about my cold hike. Mr. Gaunt was a nervous and high-strung individual who was a real "character" with few peers. On that cold winter day he stopped his car next to me as I made my way along the road, and really surprised me with what he had to say. In a very nervous and fidgety way he said, "I'm sorry, Jerry, but I just don't have time to pick you up today because I'm really in a hurry!" He closed the car window and sailed off down the road, leaving me in his snowy wake. I was very grateful for his consideration, but if he had the time to stop and tell me about it, he probably could have taken the time to give me a lift. I laughed all the rest of the way to school.

There is a ridge of land that cuts through the city of Vassar and drops down just back of where the school stood. A series of cement steps led from the upper level to the lower level. Our playground included the area above and below and even on the hill itself. One winter we got the brilliant idea of sliding down the snow-covered slope sitting on large pieces of corrugated cardboard. That was a lot of fun until an accident occurred one day. There were a couple of old Elm trees on the hill beside the cement steps. The trees had a few gnarled roots that stuck up from the otherwise smooth surface of the hill. One of the four Osgerby girls—Joan, I believe—flew across a snow-covered, protruding root on her way down the slope. A sharp knot on the root tore through the cardboard, through her snowsuit and put a serious gash in her upper leg. As a result of that incident and a few others, we were banned from further sliding down the hill.

Our farm had a large gully, or valley, that ran from the west end of the property, near the farm buildings, back to the middle of the acreage where it joined a lowland area. The valley was a part of our pasture area with steep sides that were ideal for sledding in winter. We could get a running start at the top and lie face down on the sleds as we raced down the slope. It was necessary to choose our paths carefully because there were trees and bushes dotting the valley sides. We learned to steer around the obstacles, or if that were impossible, we bailed out rather than hitting them. We wished for skis, as the slopes would have been perfect for down-hill skiing, but were never able to afford them.

Once each winter the 4-H Clubs of Tuscola County organized a Saturday outing to Silver Valley—a winter resort in Iosco County about ninety miles north of where we lived. The valley was formed by Silver Creek as it ran diagonally across the county, and the resort had several ski and toboggan runs. We rented toboggans, and at the top of the very long and steep runs, eight or ten of us would pile on. The toboggans ran down the slope on an iced track between two wooden rails and often attained speeds of sixty or seventy miles per hour on the downward run. At the bottom the trail ran across the creek on a wide bridge, and when it started up the opposite slope, we spilled in the snow. There was a moving cable to take the toboggan back to the top, but we were forced to walk up the seemingly endless stairs in order to have another one minute ride down. After several hours playing in the cold, we were usually ready to go down to the log lodge and have our lunches and drink hot chocolate in front of the roaring fireplace.

One year during the Christmas break, Mr. Heffelfinger, the high school music teacher, invited a large group of us to a skating party on the Cass River. He and his wife had built and lived in a contemporary, three story home clinging to the steep west side of the river about three miles south of Vassar. On that occasion, they had cleaned snow off a large section of the ice and formed a rink. The night was clear and the moon and stars decorated the sky as about thirty of us gathered for the party. It was a cold night and we enjoyed skating in the crisp air and later warmed ourselves as we roasted marshmallows over a driftwood fire on the river's edge.

On icy winter days, the road in front of our farm became very treacherous for automobiles. There was a gradual rise as the road approached the bridge that crossed over the Michigan Central Railroad just south of the property. On the west side of the road, there were open fields, across which the winds blew fiercely. Many cars ended up in the ditch as they attempted to make their way up the road to the bridge. Cell phones had not as yet been invented, so the people usually trudged over the ice to our house for assistance. Sometimes they used our phone to call for a tow truck, but more often they asked my dad if he would use one of the teams of horses to help them. Because Dad enjoyed showing off what his team could do, he always agreed. Dad would hitch the team to an *evener*—an oak 3x6 about four feet long—on which the horse's *whiffletrees* were attached. He hooked a chain, one end to the car's bumper and the other to the evener, and the horses usually had little or no trouble pulling the car out of the ditch. I was always fascinated seeing the horses expelling what I thought was smoke from their nostrils as they bent to the task. Later I learned that it was steam. Often the motorists showed their gratitude by tipping Dad generously. Our family invariably seemed to be short of money, so any extra cash was always welcome.

Our cow barns were unheated, but they were always warm and cozy places during the winter time. The bodies of twenty to thirty cattle naturally give off a great deal of warmth and that made the stable quite comfortable. On early winter mornings, after rising in a cold room, I would dress quickly and hurry down to the barn to bask in the heat radiating from the cows. Though they were few and far between, there <u>were</u> some small advantages to having cattle on the farm!

Our horses were not as fortunate as the cattle in their housing. Their stable was situated in the largest of the three barns. It was not located in a basement, like the cattle stables were, so it was a cold, drafty area with no door to keep out the bad weather. The horses were free to go in and out as they pleased, but they usually chose to stay inside where there was at least some protection from the winds. But, the five horses' bodies simply weren't large enough to raise the temperature of the large open-air space. Consequently, they grew winter coats. Their hair became longer and much thicker during cold weather and they took on a shaggy appearance that made them seem even larger than they were. The horses were well fed and I feel they did not suffer greatly from the poor quality of their stable. On sunny days they usually came outside to friskily cavort around the barnyard and seemed to enjoy themselves thoroughly.

We were always able to tell when the long, cold Michigan winter was nearly over. That was when the sap began to flow from the trees in our maple sugar bush. The weather was still cold, but nothing like it had been. When the sap running season began, we drilled half inch diameter holes three inches deep in each tree about forty inches above the ground. Some really large maples required two or three holes. Then we placed galvanized steel *spiles*, or troughs in the holes. The spile allowed the sap to flow freely into a pail hung on a hook below it. Daily we hitched the horses to a large sleigh that had about twenty large milk cans on it. We drove the horses and sleigh to the sugar bush and emptied the pails of sap into the milk cans. Then we took them to the farmyard where our sap shanty was situated. The sap shanty had a large, shallow tray on top of a low, brick stove. We poured the sap in the tray and kept a wood fire burning day and night under the tray. The water in the sap evaporated into steam and rose out of the pan. The remaining portion slowly thickened into delectable maple syrup. Some of the syrup we cooked even longer on the kitchen range in the house and it became maple sugar, a tasty candy treat. We kept some of the maple syrup for our own use and the rest we sold to regular customers who came back every year for more.

Winters on the farm when I was a child were difficult and uncomfortable to endure. Though they were often unpleasant and seemingly endless, they <u>did</u> have their pleasurable and gratifying moments. Even if I were able, I would not trade one of those wonderful winter evenings that found us sitting around the living room space heater listening to my mother as she read aloud to us before we reluctantly went upstairs and crawled between frigid sheets under piles of quilts in our cold bedrooms.

CHAPTER 17

THE OLD
SWIMMING HOLE

THE OLD SWIMMING HOLE

It seems that every child who grew up in rural Michigan during the 1930's and 1940's had a favorite swimming hole. It may have been a creek that was deep enough for dog paddling, a small lake, an abandoned gravel pit or a shallow part of a river with a lazy current where children could swim in safety. Michigan is crisscrossed with streams of many sizes and depths, and there are over 11,000 lakes, both large and small, found nearly everywhere in the two peninsulas of the state. It would be difficult for a child to grow up in Michigan and remain unfamiliar with bodies of water in their many different forms. Little wonder that the state has been called a "water wonderland" at different times during its history.

During the years that our family lived on the farm near the village of Tuscola, our favorite place to go swimming was Perry Creek. That stream meanders in a generally northwesterly direction in the southern part of Tuscola County and empties into the Cass River at the base of the high bluff on which the Tuscola Cemetery lies. The Perry Creek ravine separates the cemetery from the village itself. While driving on Loren Road which crosses the creek just south of where it flows into the Cass, we often saw turtles sunning themselves on logs in the water by the bridge. We enjoyed seeing them slide into the safety of the water as we noisily crossed the bridge in the car.

Our swimming hole in Perry Creek was located about a mile south and east of Tuscola near where Slafter Road comes to an end at Swaffer Road. There the creek makes a sharp bend and consequently widens somewhat. The current was slow moving and the water was about three to four feet deep at the center of the stream. We enjoyed it thoroughly and it was just perfect for us as we had not as yet learned to swim. Our entire family usually drove to Perry Creek on a Sunday afternoon and took a picnic lunch along. Summer days in Michigan are hot and humid, so the cool water was most refreshing. We romped in the stream like playful otters for an hour or so and later ate our alfresco meal on the bank while wrapped in towels. Living simply didn't get any better than that!

In 1942 our family moved to a farm near the village of Vassar, about six miles northeast of Tuscola and we never swam in Perry Creek again. However, we were not without a swimming hole. A stream called, the Moore Drain, ran across our farm from north to south, and after it left our property, flowed through Vassar—finally emptying into the Cass River on the south end of town. The creek ran near the base of a ridge of land which divided the county in a diagonal direction. The center part of our farm, where the creek crossed it, was woodsy and swampy, so it was relegated to pasture land. The horses and cattle grazed there regularly and kept the grass short and the brush eaten back which made the area somewhat park-like. One of my daily tasks involved driving the cattle from the pasture to the barn for milking, so I spent some time in that part of the farm and greatly enjoyed its beauty. I once saw a Blue Heron with a huge wingspread take off from the creek. What a sight that was! Wild blackberry, raspberry and gooseberry bushes grew abundantly in the heavier wooded areas. We picked them by the pail full, and those we didn't eat ourselves, Mother either made into pies or canned. To this day, I firmly believe that those wild berries tasted far superior to the ones grown professionally today.

About halfway across the farm, from north to south, the Moore Drain widened a little and then narrowed sharply after about thirty feet. Brush from upstream often lodged at the point where the creek narrowed and created a natural dam that held the water back. That, of course, made the water behind the dam somewhat deeper. We observed that Mother Nature was in the act of creating a swimming hole for us, so we decided to give her some assistance. We placed several logs on top of one another at the point where the creek narrowed and wedged them in place with steel fence posts driven into the ground just upstream. Then we forced smaller twigs and branches into the crevices between the logs to make the dam a little more watertight. Our engineering project worked! The water backed up behind our dam to a depth of about four or five feet and then flowed over the dam in a small waterfall before continuing on its way downstream.

The swimming hole ended up being about twenty-five or thirty feet long from north to south and probably about fifteen or twenty feet from east to west at its widest part. During the next decade the little swimming area had much use and it served us well until my siblings and I left the farm to attend college. In fact, all of us learned to swim there. We had lots of fun ducking one another under the surface, seeing who could stay underwater the longest and holding swimming races. We thoroughly enjoyed ourselves in the refreshing, cool water.

Like we did at the Perry Creek swimming hole, occasionally on weekends, we took picnic lunches to the stream and sometimes were joined by other members of our extended family at our private little watering place. A number of my aunts, uncles and cousins on my mother's side of the family enjoyed swimming and relaxing there and my dad's younger sister, Norma, along with her husband, Orin, and son, Dalton, often accompanied our family on those weekend picnic and swimming parties.

After high school, while attending college, I was home only for the summers. During those years we had yet another favorite swimming hole. The miniscule village of Juniata lies six miles southeast of Vassar. Just north of the village, on Washburn Road, was an old gravel pit belonging to the Anderson Sand and Gravel Company of Saginaw. The company no longer used the pit and it stood abandoned. Over the years the excavations had filled with spring water creating four small lakes. People from all around the area used those cold, clear waters for swimming. The lakes were very deep—in fact, in one of them there was a large submerged piece of gravel-moving equipment that had been left there by the company. We could see only the top of the machine as we swam above it. Because they were deep and had sharp drop-offs, the lakes were rather dangerous for novice swimmers. I heard of at least one drowning that occurred at that gravel pit and likely there were others.

In 1964 my dad sold the Vassar farm, except for a few acres, on which he built a new house. He retired from farming and went to work for the Tuscola County Road Commission for a period of about ten years. The farm soon changed dramatically. The house, the three barns and other out buildings were torn down. A new, modern home was built on the lot where our old farmhouse sat. The pasture area of the farm, where the creek crossed it, sat idle for years because the new owner farmed the fields, but had no horses or cattle needing the grazing area.

The next time I saw the old swimming hole (where we had built the dam when I was a teenager) was in 1990. I was living forty-five miles away in Midland at the time. One day while visiting Vassar, I decided to see what that part of the farm looked like after nearly forty years had elapsed. The farm had been a mile long from east to west and I approached it from the east end off Kirk Road near the Vassar Fairgrounds. I crossed the fairgrounds parking lot (which had once been a part of our farm), climbed the fence and headed toward the creek. The changes that nature had wrought during the ensuing years were astounding! Because cattle and horses no longer grazed there, trees and bushes had grown everywhere. What had been a park-like area now was a dense woods with trees so close together that it made walking difficult. I did manage to find the swimming hole, but only by locating the still-existing cement bridge crossing the creek and working my way upstream from it. Of course, our log dam was long gone and trees and brush were growing right up to the banks of the stream on either side. Nothing looked familiar. It was difficult to believe that it was the same park like area where my siblings and I had so much fun as teenagers.

I have very mixed emotions about that little excursion. On one hand I'm happy that I made the effort to find the swimming hole, but on the other hand it made me sad to see it in such an altered state that it no longer was recognizable. My hope was that visiting the site would bring back happy memories of a day gone by, however that proved not to be the case.

CHAPTER 18

A SLEEPY RIVER
TURNS MEAN

A SLEEPY RIVER TURNS MEAN

The Cass River is a slow-moving stream which flows through Tuscola County from its northeastern to its southwestern corners. It is the major river of the central Thumb area of eastern Michigan. Before it empties into the much larger Saginaw River a few miles south of Saginaw, it flows through the Tuscola County towns of Tuscola, Vassar, Caro and Cass City. The source of the North Branch of the Cass can be found a few miles east of Ubly, a small town in Huron County, and the South Branch has its source in the far northeastern corner of Lapeer County. From there it flows nearly straight northward through most of the length of Sanilac County before veering west and crossing into Tuscola County. The North and South Branches join one another near Cass City and from there the river follows a southwesterly direction toward the Saginaw River.

The river was named after Lewis Cass who served as governor of the Territory of Michigan from 1813 to 1831. That territory was later divided into the states of Michigan, Wisconsin, Iowa, and Minnesota. The Cass River was important during the lumbering era and thousands of board feet of logs were floated in its waters enroute to lumber mills. Local lore has it that there are still hundreds of logs at the bottom of the river—those that sank and were never recovered. The first permanent settlers of Tuscola County, Ebenezer and Phebe Davis, my great great grandparents, homesteaded on the north bank of the river about a mile west of the village of Tuscola.

The Cass River was a factor in my family's farming operations from the time my dad bought his first farm until he retired from farming some forty years later and started working for the County Road Commission. Dad's first farm was situated on the west bank of the river about a mile north of the village of Tuscola. Our cow pasture occupied a place on the river bank where the drop off that led down to the floodplain was too steep for plowing and it ended at a woodlot that bordered the river itself. My older brother, Buddy, began his fishing career along the west bank of the Cass. He used a bamboo pole and caught rock bass, bullhead, catfish and a type of sucker, called red horse, from the river.

The high bank of the river figured prominently in the earliest nightmare that I can recall. At about the age of seven, I received my first bicycle. After many spills I finally mastered the art of riding it fairly well. But the trauma of those spills must have stayed in my unconscious memory well after the fact. In the dream I mounted my bicycle at the top of the steep slope leading to the river and on the way down lost control. I remember careening down the hill, unable to stop or even slow the bicycle and seeing the trees which edged the river looming larger and larger as I neared them. The further I went the more my speed increased. The last thing that I recall from the nightmare was me heading directly for one particular tree, and just before colliding with it, waking up! I found myself lying in bed, sweating profusely, gasping for breath and thanking my lucky stars that it was only a dream.

In a much less traumatic vein, it was in and along the Cass River where I did my first territorial exploration. A very small island lay in the middle of the river just upstream of the old iron trestle bridge in the village of Tuscola. One sunny, summer afternoon my older brother, Buddy, and I waded across from the north bank to that tiny dot of land and explored it thoroughly—all one hundred square feet of it! The island was covered with weeds and low brush and didn't even support a tree but it provided no end of fascination for us. Our exploration venture didn't take very long because the island was miniscule, however at that young age we felt that we had really accomplished something. Today, when I cross the bridge and see the tiny bit of land in the middle of the river, I think back on that episode from sixty plus years ago.

Recently the *Vassar Pioneer Times* newspaper printed a small article about the demise of the iron bridge across the Cass River in Tuscola. The article explained that the span was hit by a truck in 1964, and because of the damage it suffered in that accident, the bridge collapsed into the river two weeks later. A picture shows the structure disconnected from the cement piers on the north side of the river and the roadbed lying crumpled in the river looking somewhat like a roller coaster. For over a year, while a new bridge was being constructed, the residents of the village either had to go downriver six miles to the village of Frankenmuth or upriver five miles to Vassar in order to drive across the river. The article went on to explain that the Cass River Sawmill, a manufacturer of wooden pallets in Tuscola, constructed a temporary wooden foot bridge across the river so that residents south of the Cass could get their mail and shop at the general store on the north side. A picture of the foot bridge shows it crossing the stream at the point where the tiny island, that my brother and I explored, lay in the center of the river.

About a quarter of a mile downriver of the old bridge, there were several larger islands located at a slight bend in the river's meanderings. The islands were likely formed when the waterway cut new paths as it rounded the corner. My friend, Allen Orr, lived on the river bank opposite the islands and he and I spent many hours exploring them. They had small hills, trees, rocks, sandy shores and even a tiny cave into which we could creep. We played pirates in and around the cave, and cowboys and Indians up and down the hills. We also climbed the trees and played Tarzan. Our imaginations supplied everything that we didn't actually find on the islands.

In 1942 Dad sold the Tuscola farm and we moved to another just north of Vassar, about six miles away. The Vassar farm did not lie on either bank of the river, but the Moore Drain, a creek which flowed into the Cass River, ran across the farm from north to south. The creek was in an area which was too uneven for raising row crops, so it was relegated to pasture land. The cattle drank from the creek thus saving us having to haul water to them. A hundred acre plot of tillable land was situated on the east side of the creek from the farm buildings and main fields so there was a cement bridge crossing the creek over which we moved the farm machinery and animals to the opposite side.

The Moore Drain also figured prominently in the nearly annual floods which occurred along the Cass River at Vassar. Our farm bordered the north side of town and once the creek left the farm, it ran through the town center and emptied into the Cass River at its south end. Rising waters from spring rains backed up from the river along the Moore Drain and invariably flooded the downtown business area under which it ran. Often the floods divided Vassar in two, and in order to cross from one side to another, it was necessary to travel to the bridge in Tuscola toward the south, or to one of the bridges north of town.

Harrison's Grocery Store was located in the center of Vassar on Huron Avenue, the main east-west street, and near where the creek flowed under the street. Mr. Harrison stored merchandise in the basement which always flooded when the water rose. His son, Bill, was in my grade in school. One year several of us boys were excused from school to help move the grocery goods up to a higher level and out of the path of the rising waters. It was heavy work but we were rewarded with all the soda pop and candy bars we could eat. The Vassar Theatre, next to the grocery store on the west, also suffered water damage each time there was a flood. I recall standing at the back of the downward sloping auditorium and seeing water lapping nearly at the level of the stage in front.

Though there were many serious floods when I was a child growing up near Vassar, the most destructive one occurred much later. In 1986, when I was living forty-five miles away in Midland and had just retired from teaching, I was watching the national news on CNN and there, surprisingly, was a film clip of downtown Vassar! Because Vassar usually doesn't figure very prominently in the national news, I immediately took notice. Michigan was having an exceedingly wet fall that year—in fact it had rained every day for twenty one days in succession. The result was called the "Hundred Years Flood." The Cass River was totally inadequate to contain the rising waters within its banks and consequently downtown Vassar was inundated. The CNN newscast featured Atkins Hardware, which is situated on Huron Avenue nearly across from where Harrison's Grocery Store used to be. The news clip showed the water high enough that it touched the awnings across the front of the hardware store (eight or nine feet above the sidewalk.. *The Bay City Times* reported that the water rose high enough that it covered half of the screen in the Vassar Theatre.

While the waters were at their highest during that 1986 flood, my cousin, Glenn Seney, boated northward along Cass Avenue <u>in the street </u>for about a mile videotaping the high water and the havoc that it created. The tape showed what looked like a lake or canal with half submerged homes on either side. Very few of the houses along the street survived the flood. Thus the entire area was declared a disaster area and many of the homeowners were bought out by the government. Most of them gave up trying to live there and instead rebuilt in areas further from the river. Today, when driving along Cass Avenue, one sees many gaps where houses once stood.

I read in the *Vassar Pioneer Times* recently that there is now a new program underway which will attempt to save some of the remaining homes along Cass Avenue. Under a Flood Mitigation grant offered by the Federal Emergency Management Agency (FEMA), four of the houses will be elevated about eight feet higher than they now are. Then an above-ground basement will be built under each of them. The project will cost from $35,000 to $42,000 per house, but should protect the structures from future floods. (Note: Since I wrote the above paragraph, the alterations have been completed. The homes now look very strange with their exposed basements and long stairways leading up to their front and back doors.)

Most of my recent and some of my not so recent ancestors are buried along the edge of the Cass River. The Tuscola Cemetery lies on a very high bluff overlooking the river to the west. My great great great Grandmother, Rebecca Burhans, who died in 1857 is buried there along with most of my Davis forefathers. My mother, who died in 1995, and my dad, who died in 2002, lie in the Davis plot under a large maple tree near the cemetery entrance. There is even room in the plot for me when my time comes to join those who have gone before.

Vassar people are buried in a beautiful, tree filled final resting site called "Riverside Cemetery" because of its location on the west bank of the Cass River about a mile south of town. The cemetery is situated with a commanding view of a lovely bend in the stream. Most of my mother's antecedents rest there overlooking the river which played such an important part in their lives.

CHAPTER 19

PERILS OF RURAL LIFE

Jerry R. Davis

PERILS OF RURAL LIFE

Oftentimes during the many decades of my life, I have heard people claim vehemently that they wish that they could have raised their children on a farm rather than in a city. I feel certain that they were, at least partially, implying that the rural areas of the nation were the safer places to live. It is true that such things as rampant drug use, gang warfare, drive-by shootings, freeway collisions and the like seem as if they are endemic to large urban populations. However, the rural Michigan farms of my youth, too, had their inherent dangers. Farm life was far from the idealistic haven of safety as it usually has been portrayed. The following examples tend to bear out my contention.

A friend of mine (whom I will call Carl) lived on a farm northwest of ours, and was the victim of a very unfortunate accident. He was probably a couple of years younger than I and was three grades behind me in high school. Carl's family, like many in the area, owned a riding horse. He quite often rode with a group of us boys on Sundays, when we would go to an abandoned gravel pit to ride up and down the man-made hills. One day Carl was riding his horse in the farm driveway near his family's house. He wasn't racing the horse or doing anything else that would be considered dangerous or foolhardy. All of a sudden something startled the rather high-spirited horse and he reared up with Carl on his back. A show horse that is trained to rear up on his hind legs learns to judge how high he can safely rear with the added weight of a rider, but one that is untrained lacks that knowledge. The horse misjudged badly, and when he reared, because he was overbalanced, he fell on his back, landing on Carl. Carl was killed and the horse was so badly injured, it had to be destroyed.

The younger brother of my sister-in-law, Maxene, was involved in an incident that is almost unbelievable. Buddy Cox was his name and he lived south of the city of Saginaw in a rural part of the county. One day Buddy decided to go fishing so he dug for worms in a field near an apple tree. After working for a while he took a rest and stuck the shovel in the ground under the tree with the handle pointing upward. Then he climbed the tree to get an apple. As he was on his way up, he lost his footing and fell on the upturned handle of the shovel. Somehow the handle pierced his middle and ended up going all the way through his body and coming out his back! Luckily, the handle did not damage any vital organs, and even more luckily, Buddy didn't attempt to pull it out. Had he done that he likely would have bled to death. He managed to walk home, impaled on the handle of the shovel, and lived to tell about it! The incident was sensational enough that a picture and article about Buddy and the shovel appeared the next day in the *Saginaw News.* Years later he wasn't nearly that fortunate when he attended a party sponsored by a motorcycle gang. Someone fired a gun and Buddy was shot in the head. The bullet destroyed his optic nerve and he was blinded for life.

When we lived on the farm near Tuscola where I was born, we had a neighbor named Henry Palmer. Our property lay on both sides of the road, but our house and barn were on the east side. Mr. Palmer's farm buildings were on the west side and his land abutted ours on the north. Mr. and Mrs. Palmer were already elderly when I knew them. In fact, their children were about the age of my father. After we moved to the farm near Vassar, I heard that Mr. Palmer had died very suddenly in a tragic farm accident. The incident occurred during the summer haying season. It seems that old Mr. Palmer was driving a team of horses pulling a load of hay. He was riding on the top of the loaded wagon roughly ten feet above the earth. He fell off the load of hay and died when his head struck the hard ground. Accidents of that nature were fairly common in rural areas.

Another type of rather common accident that often left farmers either dead or maimed had to do with the moving parts on machinery. I have met a number of people who were missing fingers, or even a hand, because of having become entangled in a moving belt or chain on a piece of farm equipment. Corn huskers seemed to be one of the worst culprits for removing the fingers of their operators. Probably, that was because the bundles of corn were fed by hand directly into the machine. If the stalks refused to go in easily, the man doing the feeding had to push them in. He stood on a small platform on the side of the husker and it would be easy for him to lose his balance, with the possible result of losing fingers too.

A next-door neighbor of my paternal grandparents, Lee Kilbourne, lost his life at a lumber camp located on Barnes Road between the villages of Tuscola and Millington. Lee and his teenaged son, Milton, were helping cut trees in the woodlot near the camp. The workmen cut down a large hardwood which fell against a nearby dead tree. The dead tree, being brittle, snapped off and struck the elder Mr.

Kilbourne. He was injured badly, and they rushed him by car to a hospital in Flint, about twenty miles south of where the accident occurred. He died there a short time later.

I heard of a farmer a few miles west of us who was killed when his tractor rolled over on top of him as he was attempting to drive it up a steep incline. Many of the older tractors were tall and narrow and had a rather high centers of gravity. Using that type of machine on hilly land was dangerous and could be deadly.

Our hired man, Charley Wineman, came close to meeting his Maker because of an incident involving our old F-20 Farmall tractor. The farm was divided by a high ridge of land that bisected it from north to south. In order to get from the upper part of the acreage to the lower, it was necessary to travel through a gully where we had built a very rough sort of driveway. The north edge of the driveway was directly against the steep side of the gully and the south edge dropped off sharply into a deep ditch. Because the sides of the gully eroded regularly and washed out parts of its surface, the driveway was nearly impossible to maintain. On that particular occasion, Charley drove the tractor, which had a very high center of gravity, too close to the south edge of the driveway. When he went through the eroded area the tractor tipped over! He was quick-thinking and agile enough so he was able to jump off and let the machine crash by itself into the ditch on the south. He easily could have ended up under the two thousand pound vehicle at the bottom! Later we used a team of horses to pull the practically undamaged tractor back onto the roadway. After that incident, even though we maintained the surface somewhat better than previously, I was always nervous and fearful any time it was necessary for me to take equipment up or down the treacherous drive.

My mother was a direct descendant of a pioneer farmer and doctor named Levi Williamson, who homesteaded in Huron County. The last of Levi's living granddaughters, Zella Mae Williamson, married a man named Neil Marshall, and the couple lived on the old Williamson homestead near the village of Gagetown. Neil was a quiet, hard-working man who took very good care of the family farm and the livestock on it. One day in the spring of 1954 he set out to plant a crop of oats. His team of horses was hooked to the heavy grain planter, which is called a *drill*. Neil was working in one of the back fields out of view of the farm buildings, and his dog was with him. As he made his way back and forth across the oat field, a sudden electrical storm came up. One particularly nearby strike of lightning and its following thunderclap frightened the horses and they began running. Neil fell under their hooves and the drill ran over him. He was killed instantly. The team stopped running when they reached the fence line and then patiently waited for further directions. Neil's dog, sensing that something was drastically wrong, ran to the farmhouse. When he appeared there without his master, Zella Mae hurried out to the field and there discovered her husband's mutilated body. He was one more victim of a fatal farm accident.

My Uncle Bob Williamson, Mother's younger brother, died as a result of an accident caused by a Halloween prank. Sometime during the late evening of Halloween 1955, the pranksters placed a farm tractor in the middle of highway M-81. That road travels the sixteen miles between Vassar and Caro. Uncle Bob was on his way home to Vassar from Caro later that evening. It was a very dark night and the tractor had been placed just beyond a blind curve in the highway. He saw the tractor but was unable to stop his car in time to avoid hitting it. In the crash Uncle Bob was critically injured and died two days later at the University Hospital in Ann Arbor. He left behind a wife and three children.

Not all rural perils we faced on the farm were life threatening. During the late summer we often found wild blackberries in the woods bordering our pasture. One time, while picking them, I inadvertently stepped on a bees' nest that was at ground level. The angry insects swarmed around my head, buzzing loudly to let me know that they did not like my presence. I threw my pail filled with berries at them—which did no good—and then began running. I wasn't quite sure where I was going, but simply wanted to get away from their stingers as quickly as possible. Finally, I ended up in the creek on the edge of the woods, and luckily, was stung only a few times.

Another time I had an extremely painful encounter with poison oak. Because I very rarely went barefoot, poison ivy and poison oak generally were not a problem. However, at least one time I carelessly walked, without shoes, through a patch of poison oak along a fence row, not even thinking about where I was treading. In less than a day blisters began to appear on my feet and ankles. They multiplied by the hundreds and eventually my feet were so swollen and painful that I couldn't tolerate shoes, but had to resort to wearing my winter boots over cotton socks for about a week. After that episode, I learned to recognize and avoid those vicious and extremely irritating plants.

During certain years wild strawberries grew in abundance in the sunnier areas on the edges of our woodlot. I was always thrilled to run across a patch of the tasty morsels. Because wild strawberry plants grow close to the ground, a person must kneel quite low in order to see which ones are ripe enough to pick. One day I found a nice patch of berries and lay down with my face near the ground to begin collecting them. I had picked only a few when I came face to face with a garter snake! I am fully aware that garter snakes are totally harmless, but nonetheless, I reared up and got out of there in a hurry. That ended my strawberry picking for the day.

No place on Earth is totally without dangers of one kind or another. Cities have their peculiar types of perils and so do farms—both past and present. Though I found them frightening and shocking, I had to learn to accept the many accidents that occurred on local farms during my childhood. Some of the events were funny and some were merely bothersome, but many were real tragedies that either killed the victims or left them with lifelong scars. Significant numbers of rural families were affected by a variety of tragic accidents.

CHAPTER 20

BOVINES, CONTENTED OR CANTANKEROUS

Jerry R. Davis

BOVINES, CONTENTED OR CANTANKEROUS

Probably the three most important types of farms in Michigan during the 1930's and 1940's were crop farms, cattle farms and mixed or general farms. The crop farmers made their profits from selling cash crops of grain, corn, alfalfa (hay), navy beans, soybeans, lima beans, sugar beets or potatoes. Usually the farmer specialized in a certain type of cash crop, such as grain, and primarily raised the different varieties of that general product. He might raise wheat, barley, oats or rye. The cattle farms were divided into two types— dairy farms and beef farms. The dairy farmer earned most of his profit from the sale of milk and the crops he raised were, for the most part, used to feed his cattle. The beef farmer profited from the sale of calves for veal and steers for beef. His crops, too, were used primarily for feeding the cattle.

Both of the farms on which I grew up were of the third variety— mixed or general farms. Some crops, like sugar beets, potatoes and navy beans were raised for market. However, the corn, wheat, oats, and alfalfa crops were used as feed for the different animals on the farm. We kept a dairy herd and sold the milk from it, we raised hogs for market, and we sold the eggs produced by our chicken flock.

Because of the lack of barn room, our dairy herd on the Tuscola farm was limited to about ten cows. Dad had planned to enlarge the herd and, in fact, began building the foundations and framework for an addition to the cow stable. The addition would have nearly doubled the number of cattle stanchions, but before he finished it, he sold that farm and we moved to the one near Vassar.

Along with the Vassar farm, Dad purchased all the equipment and livestock, so until he could cull out and market the poorer quality animals we had a herd of thirty-eight dairy cattle. That farm had nearly four times the acreage of the one from which we had moved, and on it were three barns. Two of the barns had basements that were set up as cow stables and the herd was divided between the two. With the farm came an old-fashioned type of mechanical milking machine that sped up the milking of the thirty or so cattle in the larger of the stables, but the balance we had to milk by hand.

Milking cows by hand is not the most pleasant job on a farm. First, the milker must wash the cow's udder and teats with warm water. Then he places a stool next to the cow's side, sits down and begins to milk two teats at a time. After he has emptied that part of the udder, he then milks the two remaining teats. If all goes well, he finishes and empties the milk pail into a large milk can and goes on to another cow. Sometimes, however, it doesn't go well.

Perhaps the cow is being annoyed by the ever-present swarms of flies that hang around a cow stable. When she swishes her tail at the flies, more than likely, she will hit the milker in the face. Cows' tails are situated in a rather unfortunate place in relationship to the parts of their bodies that expel urine and fecal matter. Often they are coated with those disgusting products which, of course, splatter all over the milker. The result is not a pretty sight, I can assure you. The stench leaves much to be desired, too.

It is possible that the cow has a sore on her udder or one of her teats. Her probable reaction to being milked would be to kick the milker. The hoof may even end up in the milk pail and then it is difficult getting it out without upsetting the entire pail of milk. Those cows that kicked regularly, with or without reason, we called "kickers." The method we used for dealing with those ornery bovines involved a device called *hobbles.* They were made up of two "U" shaped straps of metal connected by a short length of chain. The metal straps were attached to each rear leg at the hocks, which are the narrow parts just above the ankles. Then, when the cow kicked, she could lift her leg only as far as the chain would allow. The hobbles usually worked well, but I have seen really determined "kickers" let fly with both feet straight out behind them.

One episode that I had with a kicker left me battered and bruised. We kept the young calves in a box stall in one corner of the cow barn. Every morning and evening, during the milking session, we led each calf down the aisle behind the cows to its mother to let it nurse. On that particular evening, which happened to be a Saturday, as I brought a calf behind the cows, one of them kicked me in the hand. It hurt badly and I became nauseous, so I let go of the calf and leaned against the wall behind the cow. The nausea increased to the point that I fainted and fell forward with my face at the cow's rear feet. Then she let fly with her hooves! Somehow I found myself back against the barn wall when I regained consciousness. I had two black eyes and there was blood running down my mouth and nose. I staggered out of the barn and up the path to the house where my frightened mother greeted me at the door. She treated my wounds and sent my brother out to finish the milking.

Because the next day was Sunday, I went to church and Sunday school. My Sunday school teacher, Mrs. Bielby, who was rather an excitable sort, looked at me and went into a panic. She questioned me for every detail of the episode and was badly shaken by the story as it unfolded. I remember that in the opening prayer of the Sunday school lesson, she featured me prominently in her plea and thanksgiving to the Almighty.

Dairy cows required differing amounts of care depending on the season of year. From late spring through early fall they spent their days and nights grazing, and for the most part, took care of themselves. They did require fetching from the pastures for milking twice each day. While being milked, they were fed a grain mixture to give them added nourishment above and beyond what their forage provided. After the milking, they were released to the pasture and their stable was cleaned of the small amount of manure that they left behind.

In autumn, the grasses froze, making it impossible for the cows to get enough food from foraging in the pasture. From then on until spring was well underway, they were housed inside the cow stable day and night and fed hay, grain and ensilage there. They were released to the barnyard for a short time either before or after the morning and evening milking so that they could drink their fill from the large water tank, and during that time we cleaned the barn of refuse. Most of the manure falls behind the cattle in a trench called a *gutter*. We used flat shovels to pick up the manure and put it into a wheelbarrow. When the wheelbarrow was full, we wheeled it to the stable door and up a large plank to the top of the manure pile which grew larger each day. Then fresh, yellow straw was spread as bedding for the cows. Of course, the manure pile in the barnyard, by the end of the winter season, had grown to huge proportions. Daily it became more precarious to push the wheelbarrow up the steep incline. I recall a number of times when the load spilled and I was drenched. Later, in the spring, it took many, many loads with the manure spreader to transfer the accumulation to the fields. Every load of manure had to be shoveled into the spreader by hand.

Two times each day we forked hay for the cows out of the loft of the barn and tossed it through a trap door to the basement where the cow stable was located. Then we gave all of the cattle a share of the hay. Ensilage was thrown down the chute from the top of the silo and it, too, was distributed. Each cow received a portion of corn and grain that had been ground together at the grist mill. We called the mixture "cow feed." Some winters, when we had extra field beans, we cooked a giant cauldron of them each day and served them warm to the cattle. The cows looked upon that as a special treat which they devoured with relish.

We named many of our cows, not because they were intelligent enough to respond to a name, but so that we had a means of identifying which cow we were talking about when discussing them. The names helped also when we kept written records of when they were due to calve and therefore, when they had to be "dried up," or no longer milked, prior to giving birth. Most of the cows had mundane names like "The Little Jersey," "The Big Holstein" or "The Yellow Guernsey."

There were a few cows that earned their names because of certain characteristics. One particular individual we called "Contrary Cuss", because she was the most obstinate creature we had encountered up to that time. Each cow had its own assigned stanchion in the stable. They were intelligent enough to learn where that stanchion was located and how to get there, but could learn little beyond that of an intellectual nature. Contrary Cuss knew perfectly well where her assigned niche was in the barn, but she preferred visiting on the other side of the stable, rather than going directly to her own stanchion. She did that day after day, much to our dismay. To Contrary, the only good grass was that on the opposite side of the fence from where she stood, so she very carefully would work her head through the fence, avoiding the vicious barbs on the wire. Once she had her head through, the rest came more easily, and in the process she usually destroyed the fence. Then she smugly ate the <u>much</u> more delectable grass on that side. Contrary Cuss also enjoyed standing on the rubber hoses that connected the teat cups to the milking machine. That resulted in the cups coming off the teats and the machine losing its suction. In addition, when that happened, the cups became dirty and had to be washed prior to being used again. The cow appeared to have a sense of humor and I'm certain that she laughed delightedly at the chaos she had caused.

One trait that cows have in abundance is a sense of fun. Every once in a while, when the cattle were in the pasture, something would set them off and they would begin prancing and cavorting around the field. When they did that, invariably, they would lift their tails straight up in the air as they sailed around. What a sight they were!

Usually cattle are very leery of dogs because the dogs enjoy nipping at their heels. But, if the cows come across one that is unassertive in nature, then the tables are turned and the cattle become the aggressors. Our dog, Jake, was a very timid soul around the cows, and I have seen them chase him all around the barnyard just for the fun of it. He usually ended up retreating under the fence with his tail between his legs.

Usually cows are placid, dull-witted animals that spend their lives quietly eating and later lying down and contentedly chewing their cuds. However, though cattle have been domesticated since prehistoric times, they can quickly revert to the feral state under the right circumstances. The following story relates such an event. After all of us children were grown and had left the farm for other occupations, Dad sold the dairy herd because it was simply too much work for him alone. In place of the milk cows he began buying beef calves that he would fatten for eight to ten months and then sell for slaughter. In that way Dad was able to still have a profitable use for the pastures and the feed crops that he raised. At that time I was living twenty-five miles away from Vassar in Saginaw and was teaching there in a junior high school.

Home on the Farm

One fall day I received a frantic telephone call from Mother informing me that six or eight steers had broken through the pasture fence and were heading across the county. I drove to Vassar and we tried to corral the creatures, but to no avail. They had become wild in just a few hours and wouldn't let people get within a hundred yards of them. They jumped fences like deer and drank from the streams and rivers and foraged on farm crops that they found on their rampage. During the next couple of weeks we tried every means that we could think of to bring the animals under control. Dad hired a horse and rider who was able to lasso a couple of them, but still the others remained free. By that time they were miles away from the farm and Dad and Mother were getting telephone calls from irate farmers telling them about the damage the steers were doing to their crops. Because the situation seemed hopeless, Dad finally hired horsemen to find and shoot them. As soon as they were located and killed, the animals were butchered on the spot in order that their meat would not be wasted. To us it was amazing how quickly the normally placid steers became feral and in a few hours lost all the domestication that had been bred into the species throughout the centuries.

Cows are not my favorite animals, but profits derived from the herd did help provide my family with a living while I was growing up. They could be serene, ornery, dull, fun-loving, mean and even wild depending on the circumstances. The emotions that they inspired in those of us who had to care for them ran the gamut from tenderness toward the cute little calves just learning to nurse from their mothers, to fierce anger when dealing with an obstreperous kicker. Though I

183

didn't particularly like working with them, cows were an integral part of our agricultural enterprise. I must admit that I rather miss seeing cattle grazing in pastures when I visit farms that raise only cash crops.

CHAPTER 21

THE RED BULL
SEES RED

THE RED BULL SEES RED

Before artificial insemination became the usual practice on Michigan dairy farms in the late 1940's, it was common for a farmer to keep his own herd bull for breeding purposes. If for one reason or another the individual farmer did not own a bull, it was necessary for him to transport each of his cows, as it came into estrus, or "heat" as we called it, to a farm where there was one.

For obvious reasons the bull was kept well isolated from the rest of the herd until it was time for him to do his designated duty. There were three barns on our farm—one where the dairy cows were kept, another was used for housing the young cattle (those females not old enough to bear calves and therefore not giving milk), and the third was used as a horse stable and for tool storage. The bull was stabled in an otherwise empty horse stall in the latter building.

Even though we usually named our cows, that particular member of the herd never earned any designation other than "The Bull." His coat was a dark reddish brown color and he was of the Shorthorn breed, even though he had ten inch horns giving him a horn spread of about three feet. As an indication of just how tame the bull was, my siblings and I would open the small door at the front his pen, through which we would put his food, and scratch his head while he was eating. He made no threatening moves toward us and seemed to enjoy the attention.

The horse barn was somewhat remote from the others and because running water was not piped there it was necessary for the bull to be led a couple of times each day across the barnyard to the communal watering trough near the dairy barn. That chore was part of my father's daily routine. For control purposes the bull had a copper ring through his nose to which a rope was attached. Using that rope as a leash, my father would lead him to get his drinks of water at the trough. Dad had been doing that without incident for years. Never had there been any hint of a potential problem. The nose is one of the animal's most tender spots, therefore if the bull happened to be a bit playful a quick tug on the rope would usually bring him into immediate submission. One fall day in 1946 that normal serenity was to change dramatically.

My two brothers and I all have quite differing memories of the events which took place on that particular afternoon and the following is a compilation of those varied remembrances. As Dad was leading the bull to the water trough, the lead rope came loose from the nose ring. Dad retied the rope to the ring and, while he did so the bull playfully attacked him and knocked him to the ground. Dad was able to maintain his hold on the rope, but tugging on it did no good, as the bull continued his attack. Whether the bull was really angry or if he were merely being playful mattered little because the net result was just the same in either case. In the assault Dad suffered a broken back involving three damaged vertebrae in addition to being seriously gored in the upper leg. That wound was about a foot long, gaped open three inches from side to side and sliced nearly to the bone. Luckily the episode occurred near a fence, under which Dad was able to crawl, or the beast likely would have killed him.

No one was there to help him, so Dad agonizingly pulled himself upright and managed to walk up the small hill that led toward the house. On his way he met my ten year old younger brother, Dan. Dan noticed that Dad's cap was missing and that he was walking very strangely. He asked if he were all right but Dad answered in the negative saying that he had been attacked by the bull. After finally making his way to the house, we carried him to his bed, unaware that his back was broken. The family doctor thankfully <u>did</u> make house calls. He was notified immediately and arrived in a short time. The doctor treated Dad for shock, immobilized his broken back and sutured the gash in his leg.

After Dad was attended to and made as comfortable as possible considering the situation, the problem of the renegade bull still remained. We felt that we couldn't just leave him running free in the farmyard. My older brother and I (he was sixteen and I was fourteen) were designated to figure out a way to corral the animal. We knew that we were no match for a rampaging bull in "hand to horn combat." therefore, it was necessary somehow for us to capture him using brain instead of brawn.

This was our solution. We cranked up the F-20 Farmall Tractor (I do mean "cranked" because the tractor had no starter) and drove it toward the bull. We managed to run over the end of the rope which was still attached to the ring in his nose. Then we tied the rope to the back of the tractor and drove it to the horse barn pulling the bull behind. At that point we halted. We still had to maneuver the bull inside the barn and into his stall. We couldn't continue with the tractor because it was too large and, in addition, unable to cross the high door sill at the entryway. So we tied a longer rope to the end of the one attached to the bull's nose ring, took it into the barn and, keeping on the opposite side of the tractor from the beast, threaded it through the stall and finally out the hay door at the front. Then we both pulled on the rope and the bull readily came into the stall where we securely tied him to the manger.

During the entire capture process the bull never attempted to attack us or the tractor. In fact he seemed to be wondering why all the fuss. In direct contrast Buddy and I were quaking in our shoes during the whole episode and heaved a giant sigh of relief when at last it was successfully accomplished. After all, we had seen Dad's wound and had observed in a very graphic way the kind of damage the bull could do with his deadly horns. We corralled the bull only because we felt it was absolutely necessary to do so.

No matter how docile the bull seemed while we were getting him in his stall, no animal that has once attacked a person should ever be trusted again. Therefore, almost immediately, we made the decision that the bull had to go to market. We phoned Mr. Kuhnle, a neighbor who trucked animals to the stockyards in Detroit, and asked him to pick up the bull as soon as possible. He showed up the next day, loaded the animal aboard his truck and that was the last we ever saw of the unfortunate creature. In fact, we never kept a bull on the farm after that. The comparatively safe artificial insemination technique took the place of a live bull on the farm for as long as our family had dairy cattle.

Though the bull was removed from the farm, the ramifications of his attack on my dad stayed with us for a bit longer. The family was faced with a perplexing question with no immediate answer. During the next six months or so Dad would be bedridden while recuperating. But who was going to run the farm? Surely my mother would be too busy providing nursing care along with her other duties and wouldn't be able to do the barn and field work. In addition she simply was not physically able to do that much heavy labor. Another family decision was needed, and soon. It is said that necessity is the mother of invention and in this case adversity seemed to be the mother of solution. Buddy had just begun his senior year of high school and was sixteen years old. Our plan called for him to quit school and work on the farm during the year as Dad's substitute. Then he could return to school the following year and graduate a year later than he would have originally. Because of being very young for his grade in school, he would still graduate at the age of seventeen.

Buddy readily agreed to the solution and soon the burdens of running the farm were resting firmly on his young shoulders. He tackled the job with the same determination that he did everything else and was very successful. Never once did I hear him complain about his lot during that year. He always seemed to enjoy working on the farm much more than I did. If I had been in Buddy's shoes, that year would have been filled with complaints of "Poor me!"

Dad's recovery, though not miraculous, was certainly very rapid considering the severity of his injuries. His broken back healed slower than did the wound from the bull's horn. But within six months he was up and around and, by the time a year had elapsed, he was back in full swing running the farm with the help of the rest of the family. About six years ago I asked him if his back ever gave him serious problems after it healed and was surprised to learn that he rarely, if ever, even had a minor backache. He passed away in 2002 while in his mid-nineties and the long scar was still very visible on his upper leg. That reminder, along with a vivid memory of the utter horror of the bull's attack, stayed with him for over half a century. The entire incident and its results remain deeply etched in my mind too.

CHAPTER 22

HORSEFLESH

HORSEFLESH

Before tractors became commonplace, the most important power source on Mid-western farms was the draft horse. They were developed from the great war horses that knights rode into battle during the Middle Ages. Because the horses had to carry the knight, his steel armor, the weighty saddle made of wood and leather and heavy weaponry, it was mandatory that they were powerful. More recently, the draft horses on farms pulled plows, drags, and discs—all of which prepared the soil for planting. Also they provided the power for the cultivators that kept the fields free of weeds. Finally, after the crops were ripe, the horses pulled the mowers, rakes, binders and wagons that were all a part of the harvesting process. Horses were the one essential element in the entire farming operation. The two most common breeds of draft horses used on Michigan farms were Percherons and Belgians. We had several of each on our farms.

The first two horses that Dad bought to work on our farm near Tuscola were Jack and Dan. They were a team of large Percheron geldings, very dark brown to black in color. Geldings are males that have been castrated when they were young in order to make them more tractable and easier to break to the harness. Dad was just starting out in his first farming operation and was short of money, so he bought an older team that was not expensive. The horses were a serene pair that worked well together and were very patient with us children, too. When I used the currycomb and brush to groom them in their stalls, they ignored me and continued eating undisturbed. I did notice that there was one place on their flanks where they were somewhat sensitive. It was at the point where their upper back legs joined their rib cage area. The hair has a natural vertical part in that location. When I brushed across that part in the hair, their skin twitched wildly. Apparently the comb caused a tickling sensation. If I did it several times they showed their annoyance by shifting positions away from me. Never did they threaten to kick.

Jack and Dan both had very black muzzles that felt soft to the touch. I liked to pet them and enjoyed feeling the velvety texture of their noses. Also it was exciting to let them eat grain out of my hand. They were extremely gentle and careful not to bite me as their soft lips and rough tongues picked up every morsel. Both horses had long, black manes and tails which they patiently allowed me to braid. I was able to ride on their backs once in a while, too. To me those horses were like gentle pets, even though they each weighed roughly two thousand pounds and had seemingly unlimited strength. Now that I look back on it, it seems that the horses tolerated a great deal of handling from me.

Within six or eight years, Jack and Dan became too old and weak to do the heavy pulling on the farm. One would think that faithful workers such as they were, when too infirm to do hard labor, would be put out to pasture and allowed to live the rest of their lives in leisure. Not so with draft horses. Dad unceremoniously sold them to a fertilizer factory where they were killed and ground up to provide nourishment for farm crops. What an ignominious end for those gentle giants!

As replacements for Jack and Dan, Dad bought a young pair of strawberry roan Belgians named Tom and Jerry. Roan is a type of coloration where there is a base color (usually red) which is muted by an admixture of white hairs. That gives the coat an almost pink cast and is very common in horses and cattle alike. Like their predecessors, Tom and Jerry, too, were geldings. Tom was a dark roan color and was hard-working and fairly placid in nature. Jerry was much lighter colored and was the more excitable member of the team. Because the two horses were relatively young they both were rather spirited. One of our hired men, Jake Eichman, learned about that on a couple of occasions when he carelessly lost control of them. Four thousand pounds of runaway horseflesh can be frightening to behold.

I have experienced that fright first hand. My dad and I were loading hay from a loft in the barn to a wagon below. Tom and Jerry were hooked to the front and I was on the wagon arranging the hay, while Dad was in the loft throwing the hay down to me. When the wagon was nearly loaded, a small handful of hay was accidentally dropped on Jerry's rump. If that same thing had happened to Tom, nothing would have happened, but with Jerry it was a far different story. He started running. The two horses were hooked together so they raced out of the barn pulling the wagon (with me on top) behind them! Because the reins were dragging on the ground, I had no means of controlling the team. I soon realized it was a hopeless situation and bailed out landing in a heap on the driveway. The team and wagonload of hay careened down the driveway toward the steel barnyard gate *which was closed!* That fact hardly slowed them down at all as they took the gate off its hinges and ran over it. Finally, they stopped after crossing the barnyard and crashing into the fence on the opposite side. Fortunately they weren't injured and the wagon wasn't damaged, but there was hay scattered all across the entire route that they had taken. We picked up the hay, put the gate back on its hinges and finished our job—a little shaken but otherwise all right.

Tom and Jerry toiled in the various fields of the Tuscola farm for a couple of years before Dad sold that place and we moved to a larger farm near Vassar. The horses, of course, moved with us. In fact, they provided most of the pulling power used in the move. We stacked load after load of household appliances, furniture and all manner of items on the farm wagon and Tom and Jerry pulled them the five miles to the new farm. I recall perching precariously on top of a small chicken coop which comprised the last wagon load. Thoughts about the picture we were presenting caused me no little embarrassment as we made our way through the streets of Vassar enroute. The television show "The Beverly Hillbillies" with their ramshackle truck comes to mind now when I reflect on that part of our move.

For a very short time after our family changed farms, we owned twelve horses. The former owner of the Vassar farm, Bert Houghtaling, bred and raised chestnut Belgians. He had two herd stallions that were simply beautiful. The older one a golden chestnut color with a thick neck and a long blond mane and tail. His coloring was like that of a Palomino. The younger of the stallions was much taller in stature, but no less beautiful. He was darker than the other. His coat was a deep red chestnut color that contrasted well with his blond mane and tail. Both horses had long blond hair on their fetlocks that swished when they pranced.

In addition to the stallions there were six mares on the farm that Mr. Houghtaling had used for breeding purposes. They were nearly as beautiful as the stallions, but not quite so flamboyantly coifed. The large number of horses ate a huge amount of hay each day and our supply of that precious commodity dwindled rapidly. My dad didn't wish to run a horse breeding outfit, so he sold all the brood mares and the two herd stallions as quickly as he could find buyers for them. That left only two horses from the breeding farm stock. One of them was a small gelding named Prince, and the other was a young stallion named Riley. Dad planned to castrate Riley and then break the two of them to the harness so that we would have another working team besides Tom and Jerry.

After the stallions were sold, Prince was my favorite among all our horses. He was small for a draft horse and had a coat of tawny chestnut coloring. His mane and tail were a shade or two lighter. As the following story illustrates, I probably was more fond of him than he was of me. Most of the time he tolerated my presence with good grace, but on one occasion he let me know that I was being an irritant. In that instance, he was in a stall eating some hay or grain out of the manger in front of him. I started petting him from the side. In a short time he turned his head around and nipped me on the upper leg. He did it gently enough so that he didn't break the skin, but it left a good sized bruise. I understood the message and, following that experience, left him alone when he was eating.

Riley was a large horse with enormous feet. He was probably the most intelligent horse we ever owned. My brother, Buddy, tells me that Riley was the only one of all our horses that was able to figure out how to get a drink from the ice-covered watering tank in the farmyard. Apparently, he would lift up one of his huge front hooves and smash it down on the surface. That, of course, broke the ice and Riley drank his fill before it froze over again. That was a rather brilliant trick for a horse.

Prince and Riley made a strange looking team of draft horses because of their different sizes. Riley stood two hands taller and his feet were nearly twice as large as Prince's. Though Prince was smaller, he was tremendously strong and held his own very well. Riley was inclined to be somewhat lazy, so the amount of effort put out by the two horses tended to be about the same.

Once the young team of horses was well broken to the harness, I was assigned to be their driver in the fields. Prince, Riley and I spent many long, tedious days plowing the hundred acre field at the east end of our farm. We used what is called a "sulky plow," which is one on which the driver rides, as opposed to his walking behind and guiding the plow. Driving a team of horses back and forth across a field eight hours a day and weeks on end, must be one of the dreariest jobs on earth. I thought I would perish from boredom and ennui. In order to keep my mind somewhat occupied, I dreamed up fictitious people and carried on imaginary conversations with them. If anyone were to hear me, they surely would have been convinced that I had gone completely bonkers. I was desperate for human companionship and any type of intellectual stimulation!

My brother, Buddy, tells me that we had one additional draft horse on the farm for a short period of time, although I don't remember him. Apparently his name was Joe, and he was far from satisfactory as a work horse. He was rather unwilling to do much heavy labor and balked repeatedly. One added drawback about the horse was that his name rhymed with "Whoa." Therefore he stopped immediately when anyone called his name. Fortunately Dad hadn't paid very much for the horse and in a short while he unloaded old Joe. I don't know if he went the way of the fertilizer factory or if he was dumped on another unsuspecting farmer.

Dad was very proud of Tom and Jerry, the roan Belgians, and he entered them in a number of horse-pulling contests around the county. They were always willing to put forth their best efforts and earned many first prizes. An interesting note to add here is that from the time he came to live with us, our dog, Jake, had adopted that team of horses and rarely, if ever, let them out of his sight when they were in harness. The dog insisted on accompanying Tom and Jerry at every horse-pulling contest, too. He was equally as proud as Dad of the team when they won, and appeared to commiserate with them when they lost.

My brother, Dan, who is four years my junior, dreamed as a child of being a cowboy. He had most of the accouterments—a Stetson hat, a kerchief, boots, a leather belt with a large silver buckle and a holster with toy pistols and bullets. The only items that he lacked were a riding horse and saddle. He talked of little else for a long time. Money was scarce in our family and Dad wasn't willing to part with the amount that it would take to buy unnecessary luxury items of that sort. So, my Uncle Maurice, Dad's older brother, came to the rescue. One summer day he pulled in the driveway with a horse trailer attached to his car. Inside was a black quarter horse named Rocky with a beautiful leather saddle and matching bridle. It was a gift for Dan who was mightily thrilled. In fact, all of us were excited because we knew that we would be able to ride the horse too.

I have a photograph, probably taken about 1947, that shows Dan, in all his cowboy attire, sitting in the saddle on Rocky's back. He appears to be a very happy and proud boy whose every dream has been fulfilled. Rocky was a part of our farm family for a number of years. I recall riding him on Sunday afternoons with several other neighborhood boys who also had horses. Usually, we would head for an old abandoned gravel pit and play cowboys and Indians up and down the man-made hills and valleys. Rocky was a good horse and was tractable as long as he was ridden regularly. However, if a week went by without one of us taking him out for a hard ride, he became very skittish. He would jump at the slightest noise or movement and, if we weren't watchful, he would unseat us. I suspect he did that to annoy us. When ridden regularly, nothing could disturb his equanimity.

Large, noisy, gas-guzzling tractors have now taken the place of draft horses on most Midwestern farms. One seldom sees a team of horses pulling a piece of equipment in a field except on an Amish farm. At one time the horse was probably the single most important animal on the farm, because without a team to supply the required power, the enterprise had to remain small. Horses were necessary adjuncts to the Michigan farms of the 1930's and many of the gentle creatures became almost like members of the family. It makes me a bit sad to drive through the rural countryside now and see tractors doing the heavy work that horses once did.

CHAPTER 23

JAKE, THE HORSE DOG

JAKE, THE HORSE DOG

Nearly every farm in the Midwest during the 1930's and 1940's included at least one dog that was almost like a member of the farm family. Everyone in the family circle had his or her own assigned tasks and the dog was no exception. It could earn its keep in a number of ways. For instance the dog drove the cattle as they were moved from their pastures to the dairy barn each morning and evening for the twice daily milking. Some dogs have such a natural talent and instinct for herding that they are able to direct the cattle to a desired location with little or no help from their owners.

Dogs accompanied their masters as they hunted for pheasants, quail, rabbits and squirrels. They located the prey animals or birds and then retrieved them after they had been shot. The dogs used their hunting skills in the farmyard by keeping the varmint population under control. They dispatched mice, rats, chipmunks, weasels, moles and even snakes, plus a plethora of other creatures that ran rampant on farms. Occasionally they had the misfortune to run afoul of a skunk, with disastrous results, for both the dogs and the unfortunate family members who had to bathe them in order to help eliminate the odor. I recall doing that distasteful chore a number of times.

For children who lived on farms, the dog served as a protector from both wild and domesticated animals and, more importantly, from strangers who happened by. I know of one family pet that would snarl and growl at his owner when the man was attempting to reprimand his own child. Farm living was a lonely existence for many children and the family dog stepped into the breach to provide much needed company when no other playmates or companions were available. Indeed, the dog was an integral part of the family.

We had two dogs on our farm while I was a child; each at separate times. The first of them was a cocker spaniel named "Tippy." Tippy was practically all black but had a tiny bit of white at the very end of his tail—thus the name. We bought him as a puppy from a neighbor who lived several miles northwest of our farm. Over sixty years later I still remember the evening that we went to pick him up. My dad, who apparently was in a playful mood, accelerated his new, black 1938 Plymouth to sixty miles per hour on a lonely, straight stretch of Richville Road. In the 1930's autos were not what they are today, and that was the first time I had ever traveled so fast. It was so exciting that the memory stays with me after all those years.

Tippy was a good and faithful pet and lived up to all our expectations of what a farm dog should be. He herded the cows, hunted with my dad, diminished the snake and rodent population around the farm yard and helped to make us children less lonely and more secure. We loved Tippy to distraction and thought that he would be with us forever. However, to our dismay forever lasted only about six years. On a hot summer day in 1944 he failed to appear when we called him. We searched everywhere for him. After Tippy had been gone for a few days, we found his broken body near the Michigan Central Railroad track that skirted the southern edge of our farm. We speculated that he had met his demise by chasing a train for sport and somehow managing to get under its wheels.

Because Tippy was like a member of the family, we grieved for him and suffered greatly from his loss. Animal deaths were fairly common occurrences on a farm and we had become hardened to them, but the passing of a family dog was a different matter entirely. It was a cause for mourning. However, all of the duties that Tippy did on the farm still needed doing, so we put our grieving aside and began a search for his replacement.

My aunt and uncle, Florence and Howard Baldwin who lived about five miles away, owned a female beagle hound named "Sis." Sis was the usual beagle colors—tan, black and white. About a year before that she had become pregnant by an unknown and transient male dog (probably a golden labrador retriever). The only issue from that mating was a very large tawny colored male pup named "Jake." Jake was nearly twice the size of his mother and had inherited a few of the hound characteristics—a long muzzle, floppy ears and big feet. Uncle Howard said that we could have the yearling pup if we would come and get him. That was by far the best deal available, and we did so.

Tippy always had been the quintessential farm dog, but Jake turned out to be something far different. The first time that my dad took him into the farmyard to teach him to herd the cattle he acted very frightened. Some of the cows, curious about anything new, chased him all over the enclosure trying to get a better look at him. Jake never learned that all he had to do was bark at the cows and occasionally nip at their heels and they would have submitted meekly and allowed him to drive them anywhere. Cattle are innately timid and easily "cowed." Jake was either unable or unwilling to assert himself with them, consequently, as a herder he was an utter failure.

As a watchdog providing security for the farm Jake was no better. Many times I've seen him back down or turn away when a visiting dog barked at him *on his own turf.* Usually dogs are rather aggressive and hostile when they are challenged while protecting their home area, but not Jake. My dad told me of one instance where Jake surprisingly did assert himself up to a point. My Uncle Clinton, Dad's younger brother, once brought his little dog. Pete, with him when he was visiting. Pete, who probably weighed only a fifth of what Jake did, began barking the moment that he got out of my uncle's car. He continued yapping and ran aggressively over to Jake who tried to ignore him by turning away. The smaller dog kept up the noisy attack. Finally Jake became fed up with the little pest. He put his huge front paws on top of the vociferous intruder, held him down and barked at him. Because he was so much larger than Pete, he was able to hold him down easily. Apparently his action frightened the interloper because he left Jake alone after that.

Though Jake had a number of failings he had one all consuming passion. He doted on one of our teams of horses. My late mother, who loved to write short stories about the farm, titled the one about Jake, "The Dog That Owned a Team of Horses" and I have used some of the information from her short story for this narrative. Apparently Jake only liked the two horses as a team, because I never saw him spending any time in the pasture with them when they were off duty and without their harnesses. He showed little interest too in the sorrel colored Belgian team (Prince and Riley) that I often drove. But he was avid about <u>always</u> wanting to be with Tom and Jerry when they were teamed up and working either on or off our farm.

If the horses were pulling a plow or some other type of implement, Jake was there walking just far enough in front of their hooves so that he wasn't struck. He used his tail to help judge the correct safe distance. On rare occasions he misjudged and his tail was grazed by a flying hoof. Jake even accompanied the team when my dad loaned the horses out to a neighbor. He ignored all of Dad's calls to come back as the neighbor drove the team out the driveway and down the road. He stayed with Tom and Jerry all day and returned home with them that evening.

Jake, in his obsession with the team of horses, showed courage, determination and cunning—all of which he lacked when dealing with the cattle. The following anecdote illustrates the great lengths to which he went in order to be with the team. Horses that are driven on hard surfaces, such as pavements, need to be shod in order to protect their hooves. One time Dad was preparing to drive Tom and Jerry to a blacksmith shop about seven miles away from the farm in order to have them re-shod. They were pulling the farm wagon on which he was riding. Dad wanted Jake to stay behind because of the long distance, so he had Mother lock the dog in the house. Jake sensed that something was happening that he wasn't a part of and became extremely edgy and nervous. He paced from one screened door to the other trying to see what was occurring, but to no avail. Finally, after he had been inside for almost a half hour, his frustration overcame him and he went out *through the screened door!* He tracked the horses using their scents and located them before they had gone more than a few miles down the road. Jake trudged happily with the horses and after they were shod he allowed Dad to lift him on to the wagon for the long ride home. He was content because he was with the team.

Jake was struck by our red farm truck on another occasion simply because he insisted on being with Tom and Jerry. The team was working across the road in front of our house, and Jake was in the front yard. One of my brothers was driving the horses and Dad was at the wheel of the truck. He was unable to stop in time when Jake dashed across the road in the truck's path. Its right front fender hit him. Jake was injured, but not badly enough to keep him from accompanying the horses that day. He had to endure a lot of pain but in spite of that he stayed with them.

I am unable to remember just how Jake met his end, but it was well before the horses, Tom and Jerry, passed on. That was a very lucky thing as he never would have survived without them as companions. Jake, though he wasn't what would be called a good farm dog, certainly should be numbered among the real "characters" that we had on our farm.

CHAPTER 24

THE FARM CANNIBALS

Jerry R. Davis

THE FARM CANNIBALS

Our farming enterprise always included a flock of chickens. They supplied our family table with eggs and a large part of the fresh meat that we ate. For the most part, we marketed the eggs produced by the flock, but occasionally sold a few of the chickens to customers who wanted them for their flesh. Because farming is a seasonal business, income varies according to the time of the year. One of the distinct advantages of having a mixed or general type of farm is that there is income year-round. A herd of dairy cattle provides income throughout the entire year and a flock of chickens does too.

Several different major breeds of chickens were raised on Michigan farms in the 1930's and the 1940's, among them were the Plymouth Rocks, Leghorns, New Hampshires, Rhode Island Reds and Wyandottes. On our farm we raised a breed called Barred Plymouth Rocks. There are two breeds of Plymouth Rocks—White and Barred. The White Plymouth Rocks are self-explanatory, but the Barred have narrow stripes of black over a background of white that gives them a mottled gray appearance. They have bright red combs, wattles and ear lobes, and have yellow beaks and legs. The Barred Rocks are known for both their egg-laying and meat-producing abilities.

Very early in the spring of the year, Dad would buy about 300 day-old baby chicks from the Amstutz Hatchery in nearby Frankenmuth, Michigan. We kept the tiny chicks in a small, well-insulated chicken coop called the "brooder house" for approximately the first two months of their lives. Baby chickens are very susceptible to temperature changes and constantly must be kept warm for at least the first seven or eight weeks. The device for keeping them at the proper temperature was called a *brooder*. It was a large round hood about six to eight inches off the floor. The air under the hood was electrically heated to provide the chicks with needed warmth. They clustered under the brooder most of the time that they weren't eating or drinking from receptacles on the straw-covered cement floor near the hood. I remember that we had to be very careful not to make any quick movements with our bodies or hands while we were refilling the chicken feed and water containers, because chickens are extremely flighty creatures and will panic at the slightest alarm. When frightened, they would mass together in a corner and almost invariably some would die in the crush.

Baby chicks are very cute and cuddly during their first few weeks of life. But, in a short time, they begin to lose their baby fuzz and start to sprout feathers here and there. From then until they are nearly fully-feathered, they are gawky and homely creatures, always looking as though they have been partially plucked. One easily can see how the story "The Ugly Duckling" came to be written. Though the decidedly unlovely immature chicks certainly do not develop into graceful swans when they become adults, they do become much more attractive after they have grown their full coats of feathers. Their metamorphosis is impressive nonetheless.

By the time that the chickens are about two months old, the weather is usually warm enough and they are mature enough so that they can spend some of their time out-of-doors. The brooder is then put away for next year's use. The *pullets* (those females not yet old enough to lay eggs) would then spend the summer eating and preparing for their egg-laying careers. In the fall Dad would move them to the larger chicken coop where the mature layers were housed and the pullets would become full-fledged producing hens.

Normally chickens lay most of their eggs during daylight hours. Since Michigan winters are usually long and have many dark and overcast days, it is necessary for chicken farmers to fool their hens into laying more eggs. They do that by leaving the chicken coop lights on twenty-four hours a day. The hens, not being overly bright, think that it is daylight any time they aren't sleeping and continue laying eggs day and night. Chickens sleep with their heads under one of their wings, so the light doesn't keep them from their usual amount of undisturbed sleep, but when they are awake, they tend to the business of producing. The small amount that the farmers spend for additional electricity was more than made up by the increased egg production.

Another method that farmers used to fool their hens into producing more eggs was by placing manufactured porcelain eggs in the nests. To the hen, laying eggs, was attempting to raise a brood of young chickens. The reasoning was that when she saw one egg already in the nest, she would be more willing to add another to it. I don't know if any scientific research has been done that either proves or disproves that hypothesis, but I do know that at one time, it was a common practice among chicken farmers in the Midwest. Once in a while, I still see those old porcelain eggs for sale in antique shops around the country.

Chickens are the only farm creatures I know of that are cannibalistic in nature. If they see that one of their number is weaker, they will peck at that unfortunate one any time that it attempts to eat or drink from the food and water receptacles. Sometimes, they will gang up on the weakling and chase it around the coop or chicken yard until it finally drops from exhaustion or loss of blood. I have seen some of the poor creatures with gaping wounds that had been inflicted by others in the flock. Very rarely do the weaker chickens live to adulthood. The majority group seems innately unable to tolerate any disability or frailty among its ranks and tries to do away with it as quickly as possible. Plus, they get some tasty flesh to eat in the grisly process. I'll likely be called a punster, but I must say that the chickens practice "fowl" play!

Chicken coops, like all farm animal dwellings, required regular cleaning. The coops were usually cleaned out twice each year—once in the fall and once in the spring. During the intervening months the manure built up considerably and it usually took several loads with the manure spreader to empty out the accumulation. The chickens slept on raised, slatted structures called *roosts* that were set on level platforms. Their droppings fell behind them on those platforms. The roosts could be lifted off, thus exposing the flat platforms for fairly easy cleaning. The only real problem was the smell! I am no expert in the field, but it is my considered opinion that chicken manure is the rankest of all the different animal manures found on a farm. The only one, in my opinion, that even comes close is human fecal matter from beneath the privy. I would rate the various animal wastes on our farm from least to most obnoxious to my olfactory sensibilities in the following order: horse manure, cow manure, pig manure, human excrement and finally chicken manure!

Fried chicken was enjoyable and delicious to eat once it was served at the table with all the accompanying side dishes and relishes. However, getting the cooked chicken to that table was another matter entirely. First the unfortunate bird was selected from the rest of the flock. We used a chicken catcher for the capture. The catcher was a long wire with a handle on one end and a sharp bend forming a hook on the opposite end. The hook was looped around the lower leg, just above the toes and it incapacitated the bird . Then the chicken was ignominiously carried upside down by both legs to the chopping block. The bird was held firmly by the legs and wings (so they wouldn't flap) and its head was chopped off with an ax. The chicken usually was let go at that point and it would flop, spin and shake and grovel until it used up its last bit of energy and finally lay still. Next the headless bird was dunked in boiling water to loosen the feathers making it much easier to pluck. I will never forget the pungent aroma given off by those boiled feathers as they were pulled off by the handful. After plucking, the chicken required "cleaning." That process involved cutting into the body cavity, removing the various organs, cutting the chicken into parts and then carefully washing all the parts in clean, hot water.

My mother had several methods of cooking chicken, but the one I remember best is the one she called "southern fried chicken." Since that time I have described it to a number of Southerners and their invariable response was, "That's not southern fried chicken!" I'm not certain what the correct name should be, but I thought that it was very tasty and would love to have some right now. Mother boiled the chicken parts in a covered pot until they were nearly cooked through, then she rolled them in flour and fried the pieces on top of the range in a pan with some water in the bottom so they wouldn't scorch. When they were golden brown they were ready to serve, and as far as I was concerned, they were fit for a king. As I relished the delicious taste of the chicken, I could forget momentarily all the distasteful things that had to be done in order to bring it to our table. Obviously, I was not cut out to be a farmer, of the chicken variety or any other.

When my parents sold the farm near Vassar, they retained a couple of acres just north of where the old farmhouse stood. On that piece of land, they built a new house and garage and they lived there for another twenty years. The old farm buildings were torn down by the new owner, and the lot where the old house stood was resold as a building site. Presently, a modern house stands there.

Only one of the buildings from the original farmstead remains to the present—the chicken house. It is situated at the back of the few acres that Mother and Dad retained. Dad used that coop as a storage building for his gardening tools and supplies for the remaining years that they lived there. All I need to do is walk near the old chicken coop to be reminded of the hundreds of chickens that lived there, the many eggs they laid, and the work I did in caring for them. I even can remember the pungent aroma of the chicken manure!

CHAPTER 25

PIGS, PIGS, PIGS

PIGS, PIGS, PIGS

From the time I can first remember, we always had at least a few hogs on our farm. Some of them were raised for our own family's food and the rest were sold on the open market to add to the farm income. Hogs are among the most efficient of all the animals found on a mixed type of farming enterprise. They get much of their nourishment from foraging, they eat all types of household food scraps—both meat and vegetable, and they become mature enough for slaughter within six to seven months from birth. In most cases, the boars and sows that are kept on the farm beyond that age are used for breeding purposes. The hog's breeding habits, too, are extremely efficient. The sows can be mated when they are only eight months old. They carry their young a little less than four months before giving birth and have, on the average, from eight to twelve piglets in a litter. Plus, they usually have two litters each year. Some sows have been known to produce five litters in two years and have as many as twenty-seven piglets in one litter! That kind of procreativity is very impressive.

Many breeds of hogs were raised in the Midwest during the 1930's and 1940's when I was a child. They included Berkshires, Yorkshires, Poland Chinas, Hampshires, Durocs and Chester Whites. The two breeds that I remember best on our farm were Poland Chinas and Durocs. I'm not certain how the Poland China pigs got their name. When we raised them, I always assumed that they were developed either in Poland or in China, but while doing background reading for this book, I discovered that the breed originated in Ohio in the 1880's. Perhaps they were developed by cross-breeding hogs from the two different countries. Poland Chinas are predominantly black, but have white snouts, tails, feet and lower legs. Their ears droop rather than stand upright like Yorkshire's and Berkshire's do. The breed fattens rapidly and the pigs are ready for market in a relatively short time. The Durocs are bright red in color and tend to be leaner than the Poland China hogs. They are considered *bacon-type*, as opposed to *fat-type* hogs. They also have drooping ears and are known for having large litters.

Birthing or *farrowing* time was always exciting for us. As the sow became fatter and fatter, we wondered how many piglets she would have in the new litter. The nearer she came to the delivery date, the more trouble she had moving her huge bulk around on her short legs. The last few days before giving birth, she only got up to eat or drink from the nearby receptacles. After the baby pigs were born they needed protection from their mother because of her size. The piglets usually weighed about two pounds at birth, but the sow might weigh as much as six hundred pounds, and when she would lie down the babies had to have a safe place to go so that they weren't crushed. We put barriers along the sides of the birthing house through which the piglets could escape, and the barriers prevented the sow from lying against the walls.

In 1943, when I was eleven years old and in the seventh grade, I learned just how little others shared my excitement over events which happened on our farm. Our brood sow had thirteen piglets over the weekend, and I could hardly contain myself until Monday when I could relate the fact in my favorite class. Because I was very interested in drawing, I was taking a specialized art class, along with six other students, taught by a Miss Simpson. On Monday morning I rushed into class and grandly announced that our sow had "farrowed!" Neither Miss Simpson, nor the other six class members, even knew what I was talking about. After I explained what "farrowed" meant, they all looked at me as if I had two heads. "What in the world was I so excited about?" was their unanimous reaction. "So, the old sow had thirteen pigs—so what?" I was not only crushed at their lack of interest, but was embarrassed because they clearly indicated that they thought I was being silly. I have to add that Miss Simpson's attitude seemed nearly the same as the students', and that was particularly disappointing to me. Their reactions, I'm certain, encouraged me to retreat even further into my own shell and added to my feelings of insecurity. I learned to quell my enthusiasm in school about seemingly noteworthy happenings on the farm.

That same year (1943) I raised my first hog as part of a project for the 4-H Club. The pig was a Poland China barrow (castrated male), and I named him "Cho-lin", because I thought he was oriental in derivation. He was born in the spring and I fed and pampered him through the summer and early fall. Each year the county 4-H Clubs sponsored a Fall Hog Show in October at the Caro Stockyards, and I entered Cho-lin in the competition there. All the entrants were to be judged and prizes awarded—after which the hogs would be sold at auction in the stockyard arena. The judging took place in a large fenced-in area of the grounds, and we 4-H Club members used a show cane to guide our pigs around the area in order that the judge could see them well. The judge took his time and finally said, "I'm going to start with this one," and he pointed at Cho-lin. I thought the judge meant that he was going to begin the judging then, but I was wrong. He had already finished and had chosen Cho-lin as the champion pig in the show! I finally caught on after one of the officials handed me a beautiful purple ribbon with "Grand Champion" emblazoned across it.

I have a photograph, taken just after the judging, showing Cho-lin and me together. The show cane is draped over my arm and clutched tightly in my right hand is the purple ribbon. There is a somewhat dazed and unbelieving expression on my face along with just the slightest trace of a smile. Just after Cho-lin sold for an unbelievably high price per pound (after all, he <u>was</u> a champion), the stock handlers were beating him to force him into another pen, and I asked them not to hurt him. It hadn't dawned on me as yet that he really was headed for slaughter. From that episode, I learned not to become overly attached to the animals that I was raising for 4-H projects, because parting with them was simply too wrenching.

My entire family failed to follow that precept when it came to the pig that was the main character of the following anecdote. Sometimes in a sow's litter, there is one piglet that is much smaller than the others. When it comes to nursing time, that litter "runt" usually is pushed out by the larger piglets. He doesn't get the fair share of his mother's milk, consequently, he grows more slowly than his siblings, and if nothing is done, eventually will die. We adopted one of those runts, whom we named "Grunt," and kept him in a box behind the wood-burning range in the kitchen. We fed him with a baby's bottle until he was old enough to eat pig feed and he became a much-loved household pet. Grunt earned his name because he grunted when he was happy, unhappy, hungry, satisfied or merely curious. It was so funny to watch him when he became excited and attempted to run across the slippery linoleum-covered kitchen floor. He was unable to get any traction, and would sort of "run in place," instead of gaining any momentum.

Grunt had free rein throughout the farmyard, and that very freedom eventually was what caused his death. Our milk was picked up daily in five-gallon cans by a large truck that made the rounds to the various farms. The milk hauler always pulled into the driveway and parked next to the milk house while the cans were being loaded. Then, he backed around the curve in the drive and headed forward toward the road. One day, in doing that, he backed over Grunt, who, as always, was curious about what was going on and was nosing around under the back of the milk truck. I was the one who found our little pet, and poor Grunt had been flattened by the big double tires on the rear of the truck. Apparently he died instantly.

Our entire family was saddened by Grunt's demise. We children even had a small funeral for him, and carefully laid him to rest in a grave decorated with flowers from Mother's garden. That was the last litter runt that we ever adopted. Some lessons are very difficult to learn.

When Dad made the switch from raising Poland China hogs to raising Durocs, he also modernized our entire pig-raising enterprise. Just to the north across the driveway from our farmhouse, was a field about five acres in size. He divided that field into three long, narrow sections and put fences around each of them. He planted alfalfa in one of the fields, and that was the only one of the three he used for the pigs that particular year. The two additional fields were planted to other crops. The following year, the next field was used for the pigs and so a rotation plan was followed. He used moveable pig houses on skids that could be pulled either by horses or a tractor when they were to be relocated in another field. The system worked well—the alfalfa provided the pigs with forage to help supplement the corn and other grains they were fed, and their manure nourished the crops grown on the fields where the pigs previously had been. He raised from ten to twelve pigs for market each year. New litters were supplied by our brood sow and boar that we kept in other lots on the farm.

My two favorite animals on our farm were the horses and the pigs. I liked the horses better, but pigs ran a close second. They love to be scratched behind the ears and would show their pleasure by leaning into the one doing the scratching and making soft, contented sounds. Hogs not only provided us with food and income, but affection as well! They are easy to care for, intelligent, respond well to training and rarely are mean or nasty. About the only time I ever was afraid of a pig, was when a sow with tiny piglets, thought her young were being threatened. An angry, six hundred pound sow charging at you with teeth bared and squealing maniacally, is frightening to behold!

EPILOGUE

Home on the Farm was written for purely selfish reasons as I thoroughly enjoy the craft of writing. I have always been fascinated with the act of arranging words together to tell a story and writing the book was a good way to put that fascination to use. The actual composing of the vignettes occupied about six months and drawing the chapter illustrations took most of the balance of that year. I found those twelve months to be one of the most delightful periods of my entire life. Each day I eagerly sat down to the computer and spent hours reliving the joys, the trials, the tribulations, the failures and the triumphs incurred during my youth.

While writing certain essays it was necessary for me to contact relatives or childhood friends in order to check on the accuracy of, or to enhance my memories about different events. Everyone seemed genuinely interested in the project and eager to add their bit to the growing manuscript. That resulted in many very interesting and enlightening telephone conversations with people with whom I had nearly lost contact. It turned out to be an added "plus" which I hadn't anticipated.

Reactions to the completed book have been varied. They have run the gamut from outright rejection to avid interest and sincere encouragement. All of my siblings have read the entire manuscript and have given me their impressions. Several close friends have perused it and have made a number of comments. I have acted on many of the criticisms so the book has gone through a process of evolution to reach its present state.

My older brother, Buddy, was very enthusiastic about the project from the outset and had many good things to say about the end result. He went through the entire two hundred plus pages and made line by line corrections in capitalization, word usage, grammar, syntax, et cetera. He had a number of good suggestions even though the manuscript had already been proofread by my friend, Mary, who is a professional. Buddy also provided some good suggestions about the content which I appreciated. He was especially helpful in rounding out the character of my paternal grandfather whom he remembered much better than I.

The one chapter that Buddy particularly took issue with was the one in which I described our father. His memories and attitudes toward Dad were very different than mine. Buddy sent me a long letter in which he disputed much of what I wrote in that essay. Though I read his critique with interest, I felt that I had to go with my own memories of the man. The chapter on our father essentially remained as originally written.

Buddy's most helpful suggestion had to do with the title of Chapter Two, which is about our maternal grandparents. I had originally named the chapter, "Raising Eleven Children." He pointed out that I hardly mentioned the children throughout the chapter and felt that it was badly misnamed. Upon reflection I agreed and promptly changed the name to "The Jack of All Trades," which described Grandfather Williamson very well.

My sister, Joanne, expressed enthusiasm about the book the first time I told her of my plan to write it. Later she sent me a magazine article about an author who recently had written and illustrated a book about his childhood on a Midwestern farm. The description of his book reminded her of what I had told her about my proposed manuscript. Later, when I was writing the chapter about the horses on the farm, Joanne was helpful because she was able to remember the names of several of those long-departed draft animals.

When *Home on the Farm* was completed Joanne was the first of my siblings to read the entire manuscript. I asked what she thought of it and her reply was, "I guess it is all right, but you should have left certain parts out of it." I asked her for an example and was told that I should not have included the story of incest that involved my maternal grandfather and his daughter. I explained that it was all part of the story of the family and as such I felt it should be included.

After my younger brother, Dan, read the manuscript he made a couple of comments that I found to be extremely helpful. The first had to do with the chapter in which I wrote about our father being attacked by the herd bull. His memory of that incident was much more complete than either my elder brother's or mine. The chapter revision ended up being a compilation of our three memories and is a much better essay because of his additional input. Dan was only ten years old at the time and I am surprised at the detail in his recollections.

Dan's other suggestion had to do with illustrating the manuscript. My original intention was to use the chapter title-page drawings as the only illustrations in the book. His proposal was, because I described many photographs from my collection in the text, I should include copies of those pictures to enhance the written word. That was a good suggestion; however it proved to be too expensive.

My friend, George, to whom I loaned the book, read it in its entirety in one sitting (roughly six hours) and when he returned it the next day, insisted that he wanted to buy two copies. He offered to pay me on the spot. His enthusiasm was very gratifying to say the least. I was understandably flattered but explained that at that point I hadn't even submitted it to any publishers and thought his offer a bit premature.

Another friend, Chuck, after reading the manuscript, indicated that he thought the body of the text was well done, but felt that I could improve the Prologue. Since then I took his advice and rewrote it. He claims that the rewrite is much superior to the original and I agree. His other valuable suggestion was to include maps that would help orient the reader about where the actions described in the text occurred. Consequently I drew maps of Michigan and of Tuscola County, both with pertinent sites indicated, and placed them after the Table of Contents at the front of book.

Ron, one of my proofreaders, carefully read each essay as soon as it was written and offered advice and suggestions, too numerous to mention, about every aspect of each of them. His "eagle eye" missed very little as he perused each page. Ron's enthusiasm for the project was infectious, his contribution was enormous and his insights were invaluable.

Ken, an architect friend, who hasn't read the manuscript but did examine the chapter title-page drawings, gave me some helpful hints about drawing buildings. The renderings are much improved because of those suggestions.

Jay, who is an artist, poet, author and potter, also gave me some important suggestions for the drawings. The outdoor backgrounds are much more realistic because of his advice. Jay's most valuable contribution, however, came about when he noted that there was no finality in the manuscript. It simply ended after Chapter 25. That was something that I had been aware of, but simply didn't know what I should write as a finale. Through our discussions, and my thinking long and hard on the subject, this Epilogue evolved. Therefore, thanks to Jay, it is with this final essay where *Home on the Farm* officially ends.

Jerry R. Davis

About the Author:

Jerry Davis was born in 1932 and spent his childhood years on his parents' farm in Tuscola County, Michigan. He earned both B.A. and M.A. degrees in history from Michigan universities. For 31 years he taught history and geography in several junior high schools around the state. He retired in 1986.

Since 1997 Jerry has lived in Albuquerque, New Mexico, where he writes a monthly column on a variety of subjects for a social organization to which he belongs called Prime Timers New Mexico. He is a member of South West Writers (SWW), an organization of New Mexico authors. Jerry is a freelance writer and his articles have appeared in magazines and newspapers.

Printed in the United States
76275LV00005B/61-108

9 781410 779380